STRAIGHT TALK
ABOUT SEX

STRAIGHT TALK ABOUT SEX

PETER A. LEE M.D., PH.D.

Fleming H. Revell Company
Old Tappan, New Jersey

Lee, Peter A. (Peter Allen), date–
  Straight talk about sex / Peter A. Lee.
    p. cm.
  Includes index.
  ISBN 0-8007-1622-1
  1. Sex instruction. 2. Sex instruction—Religious aspects—
Christianity. 3. Sexual ethics. 4. Parenting. I. Title.
HQ57.L36   1989
306.7'07—dc20   89-33414
                                                                CIP

Copyright © 1989 by Peter A. Lee
Published by the Fleming H. Revell Company
Old Tappan, New Jersey 07675
Printed in the United States of America

Contents

Contents

Part II: Facts of Sexuality

Foreword

Is there such a thing as a Christian perspective on sex? If so, what is it, and how should it be applied in our everyday lives? The goal of this book is to answer these questions and many others relating to sexual conduct—questions that you, if you are a parent, will have to deal with as you educate your children to assure them a happy life as the normal, sexual beings that they are. If you are a young adult, it will give you a basis for understanding and enjoying your own sexuality.

Because making decisions requires some basic knowledge and understanding of a subject, part II of this book deals frankly and honestly with what were once called "the facts of life." We will discuss how both the male and female sex organs are made, how they work, and how humans behave sexually. This material deserves to be understood, because God created us as sexual beings and sexuality in itself is basically good and right. As C. S. Lewis remarked, creatures are not created with desires unless satisfaction exists for those desires. God is not a tease; He expects us to understand and enjoy our sexuality. Therefore, this book contains the facts you need to help you understand your own sexuality and to guide your children as they mature.

But knowing "the facts of life" is not enough. All knowledge can be either misused or used the way God intended it to be used. There is a matter of personal choice involved, so first we will explore the wide variety of choices available today and try to understand the scriptural truths that should guide our sexual decisions.

I write not only as a physician but as a committed Christian. Christians clearly have an advantage in formulating their approach to sex: They have a central focus, an order and direction for their thinking that non-Christians do not enjoy. There *is* a Christian view of sex, and it is applicable to our everyday lives.

I hope this book will help you think through, understand, and be comfortable with your own sexuality. At the same time, if you are a parent, I hope it gives you the insight you need as you talk with your children about these important matters.

STRAIGHT TALK
ABOUT SEX

1

Sex as We Think and Grow

Whether you are fifteen, thirty-five, or sixty-five, sex is fascinating. If you have children, whether they are much younger than fifteen or older, you care what they think about sex because you know it will make a difference in their lives. We all want to keep sex in balance. As parents, we want our children to develop a wholesome attitude about sex. Many of us have something in our pasts that made us feel guilty or inhibited about sex. We don't want our children to feel that sex is dirty or bad.

But we also are bothered by the way our children are encouraged on all sides to write off all inhibitions about sexual behavior as foolish and old-fashioned. We don't want our children to grow up believing that the intimacy and uniqueness of sexual pleasure are trivial. But we also don't want them to get caught in the trap of trying to prove their popularity or masculinity with sex.

Keeping a balance is hard. Even though we remember in part our own questions and curiosities as children, we still are likely to be shocked if we discover our children acting out their sexual curiosities. Or we try so hard not to instill inhibition that we don't teach our children the basics of sexual morality.

We all want our children to grow up as well-adjusted people— that means we want them to like themselves, to have good self-esteem. We want them to know that a contented life doesn't come from the accumulation of much money, big homes, fancy cars, athletic achievement, or sexual experience. But at the same time we don't want to deemphasize so much that we take away the motivation for achievement at school or work and in interpersonal relationships.

The secret of giving our children the right outlook on sex is to have the right outlook ourselves. We all are influenced more by what people say between the lines than by what they actually say. Even if we are ashamed of or embarrassed by our sexual behavior in the past, that doesn't mean our children can't learn from us right now. Even if there are some things we would not want to admit to our children, at least until they are more mature, we can still teach them and help them. We shouldn't get caught in the trap of thinking that somehow it is really different for children and teenagers today or that they already know more about sex than we can tell them.

Many teenagers today say no one ever told them that sex before marriage is wrong. And too many of those who heard it were never given any reasons why. Instead of understanding that again and again over the centuries the conclusion has been that sex between only two people, husband and wife, is the best relationship, teens' most common reaction is that waiting until marriage implies inhibitions.

A major influence on young people is sex education taught in schools. Learning about sexuality cannot be done without a consideration of morals. This does not mean that sex education shouldn't be taught in schools; but it does mean that that experience alone may raise more questions than it answers. It may imply that moral issues are not involved. Sex education as it has to be taught in our public schools is incomplete. It is the parents' job to put that information into perspective. It is not learning about the mechanisms of intercourse, or about birth control, masturbation, or homosexual acts that is harmful. It is not knowing how to use that information that does harm.

If learning about homosexual acts helps a young person realize that an experience he might have had can be part of normal childhood or early adolescent sexual behavior, that's good. But if it encourages him or gives him permission to try out certain things, it can be terribly harmful. Or if he learns how common masturbation is, and that it is sometimes a normal or almost necessary way of release, that can be good. But if the implication is that he should do it with some regularity to be normal, it might not be helpful.

Knowledge about birth control is important for all of us. But that certainly does not mean we have to put that knowledge to use right now. This is part of one of the biggest problems, not only for sex educators in schools, but also for those in churches. This problem is the one of the *double message*. Teenagers feel that any general statement that includes information about birth control and its availability conveys a two-sided message. While teenagers are told to say no to sex, they read between the lines that it is really expected that they won't. They feel that since adults really think that they are going to do it anyway, they need to be provided with birth control means.

This double message problem is a real dilemma not just for the teenager, but for anyone who honestly wants to teach teenagers that they should postpone sexual intimacy until marriage. You may feel as strongly about this as you feel about any guidelines for interpersonal relationships. The reason for your feeling is the basis for Christian moral behavior—love, trust, and caring for one another as God's children. We can and should, I believe, have these high ideals. But at the same time, it is unrealistic not to face the fact that some teens, regardless of their background, are going to have sexual relations. And we all have learned enough to know that we can't always tell who they might be either.

Most of us would agree that even though someone chooses to do something that we might object to or even abhor, they should not have to suffer, maybe for the rest of their lives, for it. We might tell our child not to swim alone or in deep water, but if he does, we would want him to wear a life preserver. Drowning would be too severe a consequence for disobeying. In the same way, we would not want our child to have to deal with pregnancy or sexually transmitted diseases such as AIDS as possible consequences of sexual experience.

Parents with young children then have two jobs. First, to help their children develop a realistic concept of the sexual organs of both males and females. Parents can help children to personalize this so they can feel good about how they were made. This involves some basic biological understanding that parents should first tell their children about and later let them read about. The second job for parents of young children is to teach them a personal and special concept of their own sexuality that is private. These lessons will provide the basis for a lifelong outlook about sex that is wholesome and moral.

As a child grows and his or her world gets bigger, these goals need to broaden. The dialogue should begin as soon as a child can talk, or even before, and should continue into adulthood. As children mature during puberty, their feelings give them an appreciation not only of how strong sexual urges can be but of how wonderful sexual experiences could be. This is usually much more dramatically true for males than for females, but that doesn't mean that both don't need help during these years. They should hear about the unparalleled joy of sex between one man and one woman committed to each other and the persistence of pleasure for two people who care about each other over the years. Sex in marriage should always be presented as something worth waiting for.

The Christian really has the best approach to sexuality. Our God is truth and love. Because truth exists, there is right and wrong. The right gives us a basis for morals. That doesn't mean that we don't still have our desires. It doesn't mean that we don't fail and need to be forgiven. It means we *can* be forgiven and start again. It also means that the basis of our behavior is goodness and compassion. Right and wrong, truth and love go together. It means that Christ living in us enables us to be fair with others and to not use them for sex or anything else.

Many of us tend to believe too much in behaviorism. We accept the theory in secular society that human behavior is controlled by circumstances and man does not have the ability to overcome these influences. Don't let yourself or your children get caught in that trap. To be human doesn't mean you have an excuse to be controlled by compelling, overpowering forces like sex and society. It means that we, through the power of the love of God, can overcome these forces and live fulfilling lives and help others, especially our children, to do so as well. The rest of this book can provide you with what you need as you talk with your children. When they are old enough you may want to give it to them to read.

PART I
Issues of Sexuality

2

Discussing Sexuality With Children

No matter what you do, your child is going to learn about sex, maybe years before you think it's time. It is naive to think you can wait until your son or daughter is a teenager. The truth is, children need to progressively learn about sex throughout childhood. If you don't take the initiative, there's a good chance they'll hear or see something they are not prepared for, and then, if you find out, which you may not, you'll have to patch up the damages.

Also, no matter how much you would like, or try, to protect them, they may find themselves in a sexual situation. How could a preteen find himself in a sexual situation? Almost inevitably someone, likely another child, will say something or show something to your child. It could be a wholesome fact about reproduction or a pornographic picture. A not uncommon situation is a group of kids finding a condom lying in a parking lot, or a child finding one in his parents' bathroom.

What about the family composed of an older teen and a younger brother, where the older child rather crudely describes the act of intercourse and tells his brother that he knows you, his parents, do it? The younger boy would never have thought of that. He may have seen you hugging and kissing, but the idea of you having sex is likely to be revolting to him. He may very well get the idea that showing any form of affection is a sexual matter. If that is what leads to sex for his parents, he may withdraw from any expression of affection from either of them. If you are his mother, you may find him backing away from your motherly hugs! If you are able to figure out what's going on in his mind, you can correct his misunderstanding, but most of the time, you will be completely baffled and the correction will not be made.

Maybe you have a physically mature but inexperienced daughter who goes in for her yearly physical and is casually asked about her sexual activity and even offered birth control pills. The doctor is, after all, behaving in a responsible, professional manner, assuming he has received no instructions from you on this subject. What message will your daughter get from this office visit? That she's abnormal because she's inexperienced? That something is wrong with her?

This is not to say that discussing sex with your children is easy. You're allowed to be embarrassed, in other words. The point is, you have to find a way to overcome your embarrassment and get on with the job at hand. It's embarrassing to run into the street after a two-year-old, but you wouldn't think of *not* doing it.

If you are totally incapable of discussing sex with your children and feel such a discussion would do them more harm than good, you'll have to find other ways to teach them what they need to know: another caring adult, perhaps a good book. One way or another, your children will learn about sex, and how they learn about it is important.

Maybe you're past this stage. One way or another, you've done your best to see that your children know the facts about sex, that they understand and are not upset by their own feelings and urges. There's more to it than that though, isn't there? It's one thing to know something and another to know how to use that knowledge.

If you're a Christian, you have certain moral convictions that are also "facts of life" for you. These convictions should be communicated to your children. True, some of these can and will be absorbed by osmosis, but that's not enough when you consider the other influences pressuring your children every day.

Children are silent listeners and observers of what society

considers "normal" and "expected" sexual behavior. With the current openness of the media and pervasive permissive attitudes, no parent can assume his moral beliefs are understood and respected by his children. Teenagers are no longer taught moral values in school, and all too often they don't even learn them in church. More than likely, their moral values are influenced by what they absorb from television, advertising, radio, and music. These are by no means Christian morals. For example, a majority of teenagers in one study indicated that no one had ever told them premarital intercourse is wrong. If you believe sex is proper only within marriage, you have to tell this to your children and explain why you believe so.

Sex education without morals is useless or, even worse, harmful to your children. Any discussion of an issue that involves intense interest and feelings and affects other people inevitably involves morals. If you don't discuss the moral issues involved, you are sending your children the message that morals are unimportant.

The question "What age should children be when they learn about sex?" doesn't apply in real life. It is not a matter of Mother deciding it's time Dad talked with Junior and Dad beginning his halting dialogue with, "Your mother thinks it's time we had a talk about sex."

Parents should talk with their children about sex as soon as the children begin asking questions, which will be as young as two or three. Sex education is part of a lifetime dialogue about life itself—the beauty of relationships, friendships, and families. Sex fits naturally into that dialogue. Of course a two-year-old doesn't need or want the whole picture, and parents should be careful not to frighten or overwhelm their children with facts that are beyond them. But over the years, they will learn how to think about sex and how to evaluate the motives and behavior of others.

A child will usually talk about sex if the subject is brought up by the parents, or he will ask a general, roundabout question. If his parents don't bring up the subject or pick up on his seemingly offhanded questions, the child will decide this is a topic that cannot be discussed with his parents. In addition, young children may not have the vocabulary for discussing sex with adults. The only words they may know are words they feel are "dirty," with the result that many just keep postponing their burning questions.

If your young child does ask you a question about sex, answer it honestly. The discussion should always end with your asking your child if you've answered his question and if there are any more things he wants to know. If there are no more questions, reassure him that whenever he does have questions, you will be glad to answer them. It's probably a good idea to tell the child that nothing he asks will upset or anger you. If something he asks does shock you, you should be careful not to let your emotions show too much.

Openness about sex obviously does not mean that in response to the first question you tell the child everything. The learning should be gradual. While questions should be answered completely without giving more information than requested, parents need to be alert to what is really being asked. It's common for a child to ask a related question or to hem and haw or hint about what he really wants to ask, and you have to be sensitive enough to pick up what's really on his mind.

The atmosphere for a wholesome approach to sex begins when a child is very young and is related to the child's feelings about his own body. This can be part of the message when children are taught personal hygiene. Very commonly, children are taught to wash themselves carefully—except in the genital area. Even lessons of hygiene should teach a child to be comfortable about and respect all of his body parts. The sex organs should be called by their proper names, without embarrassment. Terms such as "down there" or "thing" carry negative implications and should not be used.

The first question that children have is usually about where babies come from. If the parents have been open about sex before this question arises, they may never be embarrassed in the supermarket by an untimely question about the woman with the "big belly." If they aren't told the truth, children come up with all sorts of ideas about how babies get out. One elaborate scheme that several girls dreamed up theorized that babies come out through the belly button. According to them, the only reason a doctor was needed was to untie the knot and retie it once the baby was out. Fed by no information or incorrect information, a child's imagination can go wild, which is why parents should get there with the facts first.

The other early question relates to why boys and girls are made differently. This question is an opportunity to pass along a great deal of information, but you do have to be sensitive to how much the child really wants to know at this stage. A common question for young children is how the doctor can tell at birth what the sex of the baby is. It is hard to believe that they don't already know. It is almost as if they want to hear that the genitals and sex differences are important from day one and part of the very essence of each of us.

The whole issue of sex education can be solved in a beautiful way throughout childhood by open discussions of what the child observes in daily life. If a cat has kittens, the child should know that a male cat was involved, and how. Apples don't grow and seeds don't develop unless the pollen, tiny spores from the male part of the blossom, reach the female part. Fireflies that fly are all males, and they flash their lights to attract the females on the ground who then flash back. Done this way, gradually over many years in the context of a loving family life, teaching your children both the facts and the moral implications of sex can be rewarding for you and your children.

Talking to the Young Child

It's all well and good to agree in theory that children need to understand all aspects of sexuality; the problem is, what do you actually say, and when do you say it?

Children as young as two or three are aware of the basic anatomical differences between boys and girls and need to understand that these differences are normal. A boy is not "better" than a girl because he has a penis, and girls must understand that they are not incomplete or missing something they should have. This explanation is fairly straightforward and simple, and it may evolve into a discussion of how babies are made. Again, you will have to be sensitive to what your child is really asking and how much he is ready to hear.

When your young child seems interested in the birth process, you will want to tell him what has been called the "baby nest" story,*

25

perhaps drawing rough sketches as you talk. Although you will use your own words and tailor this story to your child's needs, the information goes something like this:

> Girls and women have special body parts that differ from those of boys and men. One of these parts that only a girl has is the baby nest, which is inside every girl and is called the uterus. This baby nest is a safe, warm place where babies grow for about nine months until it's time for them to be born. The baby nest is connected to the outside of a woman by a baby tunnel called the vagina. When it's time for the baby to be born, the woman's uterus contracts and pushes the baby through the vagina to the outside world.

Here it is appropriate to explain the location of the vagina and that mothers go to the hospital to have babies so doctors can help and care for both the mother and the new baby.

> Inside, next to the baby nest, are two round body parts called ovaries, which are little egg factories. When a girl grows up, the egg factories make a new egg every month. The egg then leaves the ovary and moves down a little tube to the baby nest. If the egg is going to grow into a baby, it stays in the nest and grows.
>
> But not every egg becomes a baby, and if no baby is growing in the baby nest, a woman's body automatically cleans out the baby nest about once a month. Just as a child's room needs to be cleaned out every so often, the baby nest needs to be kept clean. This cleaning is called menstruation, and the five days of cleaning are called a period. During nest-cleaning time, the woman's body—all by itself—washes out the baby nest, and the washed-out material, which contains some blood, comes out through the woman's vagina. This happens to every woman who is old enough to have babies, and the blood that comes out doesn't mean she has hurt herself in any way. It just means her body is working properly and keeping itself ready to produce a baby.

At this point, most children will ask the obvious question: Why do some eggs grow into babies while others don't? The answer is the story of the race of the sperm. A seed from the father has to join the mother's egg before it can grow into a baby. This seed from the father is called a sperm.

> A man's sperm grow in his testes, which are in a sac on the outside of his body under his penis. The sperm or seed have to get to the egg in order for a baby to start to grow. To do this a man's penis gets stiff and hard. When it is hard it will fit into the baby tunnel or vagina. When the penis is in the vagina, the sperm are pumped out of the end of the penis and race to join with the egg.
>
> Sperm are very tiny and can't be seen without a microscope, but each one of them is shaped like a very tiny tadpole and can swim. They all swim as fast as they can toward the woman's egg in the baby nest, and the one that gets to the egg first is the winner. It pushes right into the wife's egg, which then begins to grow into a baby.

If told this way, the child has a true basis to understand how a child may be conceived even though parents aren't married or are poor or the pregnancy is unplanned. The story can be expanded to talk about the ideal situation.

> When a husband and wife love each other very much they want to be close to each other—almost like they were one person. This feeling may make the man's penis become stiff and hard. He will want to put it into his wife's vagina. The wife loves to be hugged and talked to gently and quietly and will want to have her husband put his penis into her vagina. This is the most special and most personal physical way that a man and woman can show their love to each other.

Once the basic sex act is understood, parents can explain that sex is meant to be pleasurable and is an expression of love between married people, as well as the way to have children. A baby is not conceived every time a husband and wife make love because an egg isn't always there and ready or a sperm doesn't always reach the egg.

Facts as Protection

Young children are normally fascinated by the baby nest story, especially by the intimacy of the sex act. They easily understand that sex is something very special that should be reserved for husbands and wives who are committed to each other and the babies they may have.

Once the child understands this, it's easy to carry it one step further and explain that the child's genitals are very special and private. Only a few people—parents, doctors, and nurses, when it's appropriate—have any business looking at a child's genitals or touching them. A child needs to know that certain parts of his body are off-limits to others. He should understand that he is allowed to say no to anyone who tries to touch him in these off-limit areas and that if anyone does try, he should tell you or another trusted adult as soon as possible. If you have explained the specialness of sex to your child, this makes perfect sense to him and will not unduly alarm him. In this day and age, knowing the facts of sexuality can protect your child from abusers as well as prepare him for a happy life.

Talking to the Older Child

The baby nest story is fine for young children, but obviously not appropriate for preteenagers or teenagers. As pubertal changes begin, children need to understand what is happening to them biologically. When talking with an adolescent, it's important to relate to the child's physical, emotional, and social development. For example, you would talk differently to an eleven-year-old boy than you would to a fourteen-year-old who has already experienced ejaculation. Not only will the fourteen-year-old be acquainted with the intense feelings of orgasm he will also know exactly how the sperm are passed to the female.

Mister Rogers says that anything that is mentionable is manageable and anything human is mentionable. The aim of discussions between parents and adolescent children should be to discuss any and every topic relating to sexuality in order to establish a basis for the child's sexual conduct.

With preteens, discussions of development and behavior must come first. The physical changes of puberty, the process of menstruation, and the beginning of sperm production need to be understood. Boys must understand the natural purposes of nocturnal emissions and the urge to masturbate. Sometime before she begins to menstruate, a girl needs to know this is a normal process. She should be told that periods are sometimes irregular, that they may be heavy or light and of varying lengths, and that the discharge may contain clots. All of these events may alarm uninformed preteens and should be explained in advance. It might help parents to think back to their own preteen years and assume that what worried them will also worry their children. Many children this age will be too embarrassed to ask questions about their bodies, so parents should assume that they do have questions and initiate the discussions themselves as signs of maturing begin to appear.

For teenagers, it's important to specifically discuss intercourse. The discussion should cover the following points in language your teenager will understand:

> Sexual intercourse is the ultimate form of sexual expression and stimulation between a man and woman, the physical contact of the male sex organ with the female sex organs. The actual union involves the insertion of the erect penis into the canal that opens between the labia.
>
> During intercourse, the sexual organs are stimulated by the feeling of the penis in the vagina and the rhythmic motion of the penis and vagina. This stimulation builds to a point that leads to the ejaculation of semen into the vagina. During this act, both the male and female may experience the intense sensations of orgasm; the male's orgasm accompanies his ejaculation.

Your Philosophy of Sexuality

During the teen years, it's vital to discuss your philosophy of sexuality with your children. Although you may never have thought

of the way you feel about sexuality as a "philosophy," that's actually
what it is. Everyone has certain feelings about what's right and
what's wrong, what's done and not done, appropriate and inappropriate, and most parents hope their children will agree with them
on these points. Most Christians feel that intercourse should be
limited to marriage because it makes commitment more meaningful
and easier. Now is the time to make your feelings clear to your
children through appropriate explanations. Your influence can affect
their philosophy greatly if they understand where you are coming
from. There is no reason for a person to adopt the traditional
Christian moral and ethical standards unless they have been taught
and explained to him.

Gender Identity

You may think this is an area you can skip over. Your son has
always been a "typical" male: messy, dirty, verging on the impolite,
and quite aggressive. Your daughter may always have been very
feminine. How could they have any problems with their gender?

Although roles assigned by society for gender differences are
much less rigid now than in the past, children still learn that society
expects different things from boys and girls. From early childhood
on, certain activities, behaviors, and jobs are considered "mascu-
line" or "feminine," which often leaves a teenager wondering if he
measures up to society's expectation. A teenage boy feels the need
to prove his masculinity to himself and his peers sometimes through
aggressive sexual conduct—going as far as he can as soon as he can.
Traditionally girls were expected to hold higher standards in this
respect, even though the truth is that many girls are quite sexually
aggressive. Children of both sexes need to know that it is okay to
resist these societal and emotional pressures and live according to
their own standards, and parents need to help their children
develop these standards for themselves.

It's important for parents to realize that the whole process of
developing an adult sexual identity continues well into the teen
years. Sometime between the preteen and late teenage years, the
child will develop a sexual attraction to one or the other sex. For

most, that attraction is clearly the opposite sex, but it's not always that clear for others, and this attraction is influenced by experience. Often teenagers admit that they wonder about themselves when they learn about another teen's homosexual orientation. It may bother them if they realize that they find others of their same sex attractive.

Many preteens or teens have sensual or sexual experiences with another person of the same sex, often a close friend. Most of these encounters involve exploring their bodies and responses and comparing the results. These experiences may have nothing to do with actual sexual preference, but society tends to categorize people as homosexual because of a single experience. It's important for teens to realize that these activities, while not condoned or approved of, usually have little to do with their true sexual identification. This is obviously something that your teen will not mention to you; you will have to bring it into the discussion yourself. In such cases, it is best to begin by talking about teens in general or citing some specific anonymous situation. You don't need to know your child's private concern on this issue and getting too personal may turn him or her off.

Reasons for Teenage Sexual Activity

Teenagers say that the main reason they engage in sexual activity is social pressure. They need to hear you say it's okay to say no. Parents tend to underestimate the effect of their words on their teenagers; they may not appear to be listening to you, but they really are. Children are interested in honest, candid discussions of sex, and unless they have been given some reason not to trust their parents, they are profoundly influenced by them.

In telling your son or daughter that it's okay to say no, you have to look at the other side of the facts and figures. The media say that about half of today's teenagers are sexually active. The other side of the coin is obvious: Half of today's teenagers are *not* sexually active!

It's also necessary to discuss the usual reasons teens give for having sex. Boys generally do so to prove to themselves and their peers that they are men; girls do so to hang on to their boyfriends.

Both sexes commonly engage in sex to obtain the comfort of being loved and cared for that is a very real need for them. Other common reasons include the need to be popular, to avoid loneliness, to prove they are "normal," to find out what they've been missing, and to rebel against their parents.

Parents realize that having sex for these reasons rarely meets the child's needs and often leads to sadness, more loneliness, and unhappiness. Throughout their children's teen years, parents should respond to incidents in the media, the community, and among friends, family, and acquaintances that highlight these insufficient motives for sexual activity. Just as you wouldn't let your child take the wrong medicine for a headache, you shouldn't let him believe that sexual activity is the answer to teenage doubts and fears.

Trust

Trust is critical to the parent-child relationship, but many parents find it hard to trust their teenagers, especially where sex is concerned. Once you have discussed your sexual philosophy and the reasons you feel a certain way about the subject, you must trust your children.

After months of pressure from her boyfriend, one girl gave in, only to have her parents find out. Her mother's first words to her were, "How many others were there before this?" Although the mother had a right to be upset, her unfeeling words shattered her daughter and destroyed their relationship. Parents need to set a standard of behavior, but they must also be prepared to cope with human failure and treat it with the kindness they expect when they themselves fail. Even a child who knows he has failed needs to feel he can regain his parents' trust.

This type of trust is desperately needed today because family stability is no longer guaranteed. Many children now live with only one of their natural parents. Less than 60 percent of all families contain a married couple; 15 percent are single-parent families. In more than 25 percent of these single-parent families, the parent was never married, and almost half are divorced. Children who must cope with this type of insecurity need parents they can trust to love them, no matter what they do.

Family Openness

In general, openness about sex is a desirable family characteristic. It encourages children to ask questions without embarrassment and allows parents to bring up the subject naturally, as needed. It's usually quite easy to be open and honest with young children, but as your children reach the teenage years, it becomes a little more difficult.

Physical gestures of caring, such as touching and embracing, are important to preteens and teens, but they may be more difficult for them during this period. Teens need to hear that touching can be a way of simply demonstrating affection. Although it may in some cases lead to sex, there is room and an enormous need by all of us for affection without sex. Teens must learn that sex is not the only or best way to obtain physical comfort and reassurance. Some families seem to be natural touchers and huggers, others are not; both types may need to adjust during the teenage years. Those who do not readily physically display affection may be that way because of parents' inhibitions and their experiences when young. If parents would really like to show their love more readily, they should work on doing it and making it natural.

Young children quite often see their parents in varying stages of nudity, and this type of openness is fine, within reason. But once children have reached the preteen years, any casual display of parental nudity with children of the opposite sex should be avoided. Still, the accidental or incidental observation of either parent should not be overresponded to. It happens, and it won't scar anyone for life.

Candid discussions or comments about genital and breast size can be quite helpful at this age. Boys are often impressed with the size of their fathers' penises and feel they will never measure up. To keep this in perspective, the father can mention that he felt this way as a boy, giving his son the casual assurance that he will grow during puberty to be just like any other man.

Openness within the family about sexuality should not include any details of parental sexual activity, which should be kept private. Children often accidentally observe or hear their parents having sex, and the initial reaction can be one of disgust, distrust, and bewilderment. Even children who realize what they are seeing or hearing tend to feel angry with the father, who seems to be in an aggressive position with respect to the mother.

If seeing the act of intercourse between parents in a stable family is traumatic to children, imagine the child's impression when seeing a parent having sex with someone from outside the family. This happens with increasing frequency today. For the child's sake it shouldn't happen and is just one of the host of reasons related to trustworthiness for limiting sex to marriage.

While seeing parents having intercourse is traumatic, it is not necessarily disastrous. Children in concentration camps during the Second World War lived without privacy, often seeing their parents and others having sex. This may even have taught them something about the comfort of the sex-marriage commitment during times of hopeless disaster.

Each child needs to know that all humans have sexual desires and appetites that are normal, not wrong. However, he also needs to know that it is only when people govern those desires that they can become a unique, special bond between husband and wife, while at the same time being immensely pleasant and enjoyable.

* Adapted with permission from the sex education story in "Sex Errors of the Body" by John Money, The Johns Hopkins University Press, Baltimore, Md. Copyright © 1968

3

Sexual Behavior in Children and Teenagers

Parents often deny to themselves that all humans—more specifically their children—are naturally curious about sex and that sexual play of an exploratory nature is common. This denial is, of course, an unrealistic reaction that lets parents avoid facing what may be uncomfortable facts. Either that or the parents are very naive or uninformed. But there is nothing in Christian teaching or Scripture that suggests Christians should be naive or uninformed. Neither does Scripture urge Christians to avoid reality. In fact, it does just the opposite. Ignorance is not bliss; what you don't know can hurt you.

The following discussion of human sexual behavior is simply a description of humanity, which was created by God with natural sexual curiosity, desires, and drives. What humanity, what each person does with these facts is what's important. Scripture certainly provides ample guidance on these points, and parents have the obligation to pass this guidance on to their children in a loving, understanding manner, but it is unrealistic to ignore the basic nature of humanity and natural curiosity of a child.

Sexual Responses

Sexual interest, feelings, and responses clearly exist long before pubertal growth and its hormonal changes. In terms of touching, even infants and small children have the potential for sexual arousal. The difference between their reactions and those after adolescence is that sexual desire does not motivate infants to seek such experiences. They usually are incidental, often an innocent result of exploring their own bodies, and do not happen with regularity.

Frequent erections occur in male infants. They are not the result of specific sexual arousal. Partial erections may occur simply as part of the relaxation phase of control muscles allowing more blood to flow into the penis just before urination begins. Genital exploration and play are common in infants and children, but purposeful and regular self-stimulation is rare. Young males have frequent erections before puberty, most of them in response to a wide variety of stimuli, a good number of which are nonsexual. Erections at this age usually come and go very quickly.

The capability of orgasm is present before puberty but rarely experienced. It's common for children to touch or fondle their genitals in the normal process of learning, or during transient episodes of self-stimulation. In this sense, masturbation commonly occurs during childhood. This, however, is clearly different from the deliberate erotic self-stimulation to produce physical and emotional excitement in an adult sense of masturbating, which is rare before puberty. Although parents are often embarrassed by a child's innocently touching himself, it is unwise to display an emotional response to it. The child can simply be told that because that part of the body is private it's impolite to do this in public. If it becomes a habit, the child can be distracted with a toy or another activity. It's certainly unnecessary and inadvisable to be harsh or to reprimand a toddler or older child in a way that could produce guilt.

At least 50 percent of all prepubertal children engage in some type of sexual play with another child. In most cases, this is motivated by curiosity and the need to compare oneself with others. This activity seems to be more common among boys than girls, since even in childhood, the male's sexual drive is more genitally directed than the female's. The incidence of these experiences gradually increases through childhood and peaks during early puberty. There is really no time during childhood when a child is uninterested in sexual matters or unaware of sexual feelings—even though he may

36

not recognize them as sexual at this age. Parents should recognize this and not be dismayed when evidence of it surfaces. A child should not be made to feel guilty because of a parent's inappropriate reactions.

Sexual play in childhood is sporadic and usually motivated by an inquisitive, explorative attitude rather than an exploiting, pleasure-seeking one. What the sexual play actually involves is related to socioeconomic and religious background. Simply put, children are likely to try things they have learned about, especially if they have gotten the message that it is acceptable and everyone does it. Otherwise their activities are likely to involve looking and touching in only private situations.

This type of sexual play is more common between children of the same sex than between opposite sexes, but this does not imply any predisposition toward homosexuality. Since it occurs at a time when children are more comfortable with others of the same sex, sexual play with members of the same sex is consistent with general childhood social activities and should not alarm parents. Generally this type of activity involves nothing more than "show me," although any type of bodily contact is possible.

Although both homosexual and heterosexual play continue into adolescence, both actually become less common. During childhood the commonest situation is a variation of exploratory childhood play in which there may be only one actual sexual incident with someone of either sex. As puberty approaches, the development of sexual behavior becomes more private. There is a marked difference in activity between males and females because of the dramatic increase of masturbation in boys.

Parents' comments about such activities when discovered should be carefully worded. It is just as important not to make children feel guilty as it is to teach them that sex is good and right in the appropriate time and place. Parents should not be dismayed nor children made to feel guilty when childhood play is discovered to include sexual things.

Male Concerns

Males at any age may become concerned about their penis size. It occurs especially at the age when group undressing and showering begins in school. Most boys this age are wondering if they will ever mature, and it is not uncommon for them to think others' penises are bigger than their own.

Boys should realize that a penis changes a great deal in size from time to time, depending on how much blood is in it. This is determined by how warm or cold, relaxed, nervous, or upset a boy is, or how hard he may have been exercising. With hard physical exercise, the body's blood is directed to other organs, so the penis will be shorter and smaller than when the boy is warm, rested, and relaxed. In addition, a boy looking down at his own penis will always have a foreshortened view, and his own penis will look smaller to him than a penis viewed from the side. Body build also affects apparent penile length. A thin person without much fat above the penis will appear to have a longer penis. A lot of hair around the base may make the penis appear shorter.

These misconceptions plus the fact that some boys mature earlier make many boys' first locker-room experience traumatic during junior high years. The less-developed boys are overawed by the more developed, while the developed boys often feel embarrassed, freakish, and "on display."

All of these concerns lead some males to go to great lengths to avoid being seen undressed. They may avoid using public urinals or carefully shield themselves. They may "forget" their gym clothes, or learn to change while hiding themselves with clothing or a towel. Such situations are not rare, but should ease as boys develop and become comfortable with their own bodies. In the meantime, parents should provide boys with the facts mentioned here and assure them that they are normal and will sooner or later catch up to everyone in the class. They can expect to be like other males as adults. It is also worth mentioning that comparisons by glimpses in locker rooms may give wrong impressions. A person who might appear to have a big penis at one moment may in the next few moments appear much smaller because of normal variations.

This period of life, perhaps the most sensitive time of development for boys, can be made much easier if their parents have prepared them for it. It is helpful to explain that all boys are embarrassed at least at first when they have to undress around others who may be more developed than they are. If Dad can share his own experiences or feelings from that age it is helpful. He can indicate that penis size in men is essentially the same but during pubertal years some boys mature sooner or faster.

There are many other body image concerns that may be troublesome for males. It is almost always helpful if a father can discuss these with his son. Ideally these concerns will be resolved by the end of adolescence, but they sometimes surface again in later life. Concerns are not always closely related to sexuality. They may involve height, body build, complexion, or hair color. Amount and distribution of beard or body hair, especially chest hair, for example, may take on too great an importance.

The whole issue of being comfortable with one's own body and nudity is often more obvious for males. This is related to the facts that their anatomy is more likely revealed and bathroom exposure more obvious. Males are likely to become self-conscious about this well before puberty. Parents should not be surprised when it seems that suddenly their son goes from running around the house nude to becoming very private. This desire for privacy in the bathroom or shower should be respected. Of course, the answer and the right perspective about all of this is that, even though both sexes are just the same, each person is also unique and just fine the way he is. Satisfaction and a healthy body image come to our children, as to anyone, when they learn to like themselves as they are.

Female Concerns

Females generally are provided with more privacy in locker rooms and bathrooms, so the trauma of early puberty is of a different sort and may not involve nudity. Nevertheless, there can be considerable concern about too little or too much breast or pubic hair development, size and shape of the labia, and pigmentation of the genitalia.

The greatest concern is usually about breast development. While large breasts attract attention, it is not always the most desirable kind of attention. On the other hand, small breasts or lack of breast development is often the cause of psychological trauma during teen years. Women looking back often say that this influenced their lives more than any other body trait.

Generally, girls can't hide the degree of breast development they have. Those who are late developing or less developed often feel that they are treated by boys as a little kid or that they are thought of as a cute little girl. It seems to them as if every girl who is asked to date has considerable breast development.

It is helpful to remember that cultural emphasis or styles concerning the female figure and breasts change with time. More recently the petite or slim figure is as popular as the voluptuous model of a few decades ago.

Nevertheless, having underdeveloped or small breasts can be very traumatic at this age. To make matters even worse, an underdeveloped girl is likely to be teased by other girls and by boys, while only in the cruelest situations does an underdeveloped boy face teasing from girls.

Differences in breast development influence a girl's clothing selection because both large and small girls have to avoid certain types of clothing in an attempt to appear "normal." Mothers should be aware of this fact when shopping with their daughters and tactfully steer them toward clothing that fits their body type. Junior sizes may simply not fit while juvenile styles are inappropriate. Uniforms and sweaters of certain fabrics may be a particular problem for the girl with a large bust while tailored blouses may fit awkwardly on both the larger and smaller.

Another female concern revolves around the onset of menstruation. Early-maturing girls may have to do things differently during their periods, which is not understood by their peers. This will be the cause of many curious questions, often well-meaning but embarrassing, some of which will come from uninformed boys. One brother was concerned that his sister might be using drugs because she would sometimes take a strange packet into the bathroom. Late-maturing girls tend to wonder what's wrong with them once all their friends have begun to menstruate. Not only do they feel abnormal, they also feel isolated from some mysterious "sisterly" secrets possessed by their more mature friends.

Masturbation

During early puberty, there is a marked difference in overall sexual activity in males and females. Boys have a dramatic increase of activity, primarily of solitary masturbation. While any genital stimulation during childhood is often referred to as masturbation, from puberty onward the definition implies stimulation to the point of orgasm. Rubbing of the genitals simulating the stimulation of intercourse is usually involved.

Most boys experience their first orgasm and ejaculation as the result of masturbation, others through a nocturnal emission. It's common for a boy experiencing his first orgasm and ejaculation to feel guilty or assume he has hurt himself, but in spite of this, masturbation is a commonly repeated act for most pubertal boys.

Girls do not have the often overwhelming urge to masturbate that boys do, although the incidence of female masturbation has risen in the last twenty years because of more widespread knowledge about it among girls and the belief that they have as much right to sexual pleasure as boys do.

There are still sex differences in the amount of male and female masturbation, but the differences have decreased considerably. Generally, by the end of the teen years twenty years ago, slightly less than 90 percent of all males reported masturbation experiences; today it is somewhat more than 90 percent. Female incidence has risen from 50 percent to somewhat less than 75 percent. Males still masturbate more frequently, from daily to monthly, although the average is two to three times a week. The average young female who masturbates regularly does so about once a week. Concerns and problems about masturbation are discussed in the next chapter.

The Proper Perspective

Sexual behavior is clearly different today from what it was twenty years ago, which is a reflection of society's mores and the influence of the media. It would be naive to assume that young Christians have not been influenced by these changes, even though they have been taught morality in the home and church.

Rather than shuddering about the horrors of sexual immorality, parents need to define—for themselves and their children—ways to avoid them and the things that are likely to have an unhealthy influence. There is a difference between the immoral and the undesirable. There is a difference between something that is clearly immoral and something that might lead to immorality. While neither may be desirable, there is room for understanding and education in the case of anything that is not in itself immoral. This can include the way one dresses, where to go for social functions, whom to go with, and how much time is spent alone with people.

Within the principles of Christian conduct, this is a distinction that must be made in each family according to its own standards and beliefs, and the decisions will vary from family to family. The danger in being too strict is that parents may be seen as unrealistic, harsh, and unhelpful with the problems and pressures of sexual behavior. Being too lenient includes the risk of leaving children with no values at all to use as an anchor in a confused world.

Meanwhile, other influences today are shortening childhood and adolescence, forcing young people to grow up before they are prepared for the choices required of them in the adult world. Adolescents are being exploited in an attempt to tap their newfound buying power, and the commercial influence is now reaching children in grade school, who are being pressured into demanding designer clothing and jewelry they would never have asked for on their own.

In spite of movie ratings and TV warnings, the mysteries of growing up or adulthood are conspicuously teasing even the youngest child. The preteen group may be the most influenced. This group includes some of the most avid followers of clothing trends and most eager fans of entertainers, such as rock stars. Their influence leads not only children but also adults to view adult actions and behaviors as things to attain as quickly as possible.

Dangers of Sexual Abuse

As part of this new view of childhood, more and more adults are seeing children as sexual beings able to participate in adult concepts of sexuality. This fact is clearly related to the increased incidence of child molestation. Not only is the child naturally curious about sex, but this curiosity has been heightened by the movies, TV shows, and reading material generally available to him, which gives him a dangerously more vulnerable quality. All this also makes the adult perpetrator bolder.

Many children, both boys and girls, are victims of sexual abuse. This is usually but not always inflicted by a teenage or adult male and usually involves the adult showing himself, looking at the child's genitals, and sometimes touching. Sadly it may involve much more than that. If it is a single experience, realistic, loving counseling by parents may be adequate and psychological consequences may be avoided. However, these situations should not be hushed up. They need to be talked about within the privacy of the family. If the incident continues to be disturbing or if more than looking or touching was involved, or if it happens more than once, professional counseling is needed.

Because sexual play in childhood is sporadic and usually motivated by an inquisitive, explorative attitude rather than a pleasure-seeking one, parents should be alerted if behavior or attitudes seem inappropriate for the child's age. Regular self-stimulation, especially if to the point of orgasm, may be evidence that this has been taught, not self-discovered. Such inappropriate behavior may be because of activities with or observations of such activities by older persons.

Because even a young child has the potential for sexual arousal, children of any age are potential victims of abuse and molestation. Child molesters may be family members or friends. It is almost always someone who has developed a relationship with the child and established trust. He spends time with the child and often shares secrets. At first the secrets are harmless but they lay the groundwork for future sexual secrets. Pornography is often introduced, usually soft-core at first to desensitize the child to nudity and then hard-core may be added. Seeing pictures carries a powerful message that what is depicted must be acceptable. If this scheme works, the perpetrator will eventually introduce sex acts, always extracting a promise of secrecy either based on an established trust or by threats.

What can parents do about this danger? First, always be realistic

43

about the possibility. No adult should ever expect to share privacy with a child without the parents' permission. Unfortunately, those in public trust, including teachers and church workers, have been child molesters. No trustworthy adult would allow a situation in which such behavior could be remotely suspected. Parents should teach their children certain basic rules and observe guidelines themselves. Children can learn that certain areas of their bodies are private and the difference between touching that is okay and touching that is bad. They should be assured that they should tell you if anyone does anything strange. You should always take any such reports seriously.

As a safeguard to prevent a child from willingly going with an adult who says he has been sent by the family to get him, many families have developed a secret code word. If the code word isn't hidden in the message, the child knows he or she shouldn't go. A backup course of action should be planned in case of an emergency; for example, call Grandma's house. Because an abductor often tries to call a child by name, it is wise to label clothes or school supplies with small letters in a spot that is not easily observed. Of course, parents should know about or check out the houses of playmates before allowing their children to go there. The best preventative is spending time with your children; the easiest victims for child molesters are insecure children who need and crave attention and affection.

A Healthy and Safe Approach

The proper perspective about children and sex is that normal childhood sex play is usually motivated by curiosity and generally ends in early puberty. The natural progression is to heterosexual activity for both sexes unless the teenager is given some reason to control his or her biological urges. Children need to be told that they have the ability to think through situations and control their urges in order to meet their goals, whether they involve academics, athletics, or interpersonal relationships.

If a teenager has not been taught differently, he will follow his curiosity about his body and be lured into sexual activity by the "feel good" factor, which says that anything that feels good cannot be bad.

44

This is today's message to teenagers, but it is a message that can be overcome by parents who know better.

Even while taking the position that sexual intercourse should be restricted to marriage, our thinking must be broad enough and compassionate enough to help teenagers who are already sexually active. While this leaves counselors and other professionals with the problem of sending a double message, this doesn't have to be so for parents. Generally, many people take the stand that intercourse is to be limited to marriage but also teach birth control. This is likely to give teenagers the double message that even though we tell them they should wait until marriage, we really expect them to try sex anyway. Being realistic about human nature leaves no option but to realize that some teenagers will have intercourse no matter what anyone says (some always have). And no concerned person would want an unwanted child to be conceived, so most would feel that if teens are going to have sex, they should use birth control.

Even though this double message may be implied to teenagers in general, there needn't be any dilemma in the message parents give to their own children. If parents believe in the sanctity of marriage, their belief that their children should guard their sexuality and wait is plain enough. Parents should believe their teenagers are capable of making tough moral decisions. So while teens may hear a double message in general, even from the church, they don't have to from their parents. If parents believe that sex should be limited to marriage, if they themselves elevate marriage and sex to that high level, they give no double message. It is the parents' duty to provide the basic information about sexuality and the implications and risks of sexual activity outside of marriage, including a discussion about AIDS, and to help their children make an informed, rational decision. Of course, there is no guarantee that the teenager will make the right decision, but the influence of parents is tremendous and greater than most parents realize.

However, after a daughter is pregnant, or a son has gotten a girl pregnant is not the time to extol chastity. It is the time for loving concern to decide what's best for everyone involved. After all, the ultimate essence of Christianity is not the ability to live up to the best standards, but love and forgiveness.

4

Masturbation

The term masturbation may have various meanings. The general definition of sexual self-stimulation can apply to any stimulation of erotic areas to cause pleasurable physical sensations. A two-year-old boy who puts his hand under his diaper and fondles his penis could be considered to be masturbating by this definition. All children discover a pleasurable feeling from touching their genitals. This may be more obvious in boys because stimulation results in erection or spontaneous erections call for touching. Young children, especially boys, may lie on their stomachs and thrust their hips rhythmically into the bed during sleep or while going to sleep. Older children and adults, often as an unconscious gesture, touch or caress their genital area. By this kind of general definition, all masturbate.

The definition of masturbation that needs to be discussed is the situation that occurs usually only during and after puberty. This is the purposeful stimulation of the genital organs usually but not always leading to orgasm. In males the stimulation involves primarily the penis and the orgasm occurs during ejaculation. Female masturbation most commonly involves the clitoris. Masturbation usually includes some type of rhythmic pressure. Although techniques vary, it is inappropriate and probably unnecessary to describe them here. However, it is worth mentioning that some techniques may be harmful. For instance, inserting objects into the urethra can cause damage or infection. One extremely dangerous and potentially fatal masturbation technique is called autoerotic asphyxiation. This involves using pressure to decrease blood flow to the brain to intensify sensation. This pressure is produced by a piece of clothing or something else wrapped around the neck behind the jaw to slow circulation to the head. The terrible result can be that at the moment of intensity death may result by hanging.

First Knowledge

Young people are introduced to masturbation in many different ways.

An eleven-year-old physically immature boy from a home where parents were faithful to each other, where sex was seldom talked about but respected, and where Christian ethics were taught was introduced to masturbation in a very traumatic way. A neighbor boy who was almost three years older took him to his home and when no one was around showed him.

Another group of boys learned in a junior high Sunday school class that this was something that most boys did and that they should not worry about it. A youth group of boys and girls from a different church were told that the Seventh Commandment, "Thou shall not commit adultery," meant that any form of sexual stimulation outside of marriage, even if alone, was wrong.

A teenage girl picked up a pamphlet in the health room in her high school. It encouraged her to masturbate if and when she wanted. It implied that people who warned against it were wrong and that it could not become a bad habit. Reading the pamphlet made her feel that she was clearly missing something if she didn't do it, although she felt no urge to until she was given this impression that everyone else was.

Historical Background

Sexual self-stimulation, or masturbation, has been a morality issue for centuries, with most early writers unequivocally condemn-

ing it. The word itself implies condemnation. The term *masturbation* is defined in a dictionary as recent as from the 1940s as
"sexual self-abuse or defilement." It is derived from the Latin words
for "hand" and "pollute," suggesting that those who masturbate
desecrate themselves with their own hands, a concept related to the
principle of Onanism.

The term *Onanism* is derived from the biblical account of the
disobedient behavior of Onan (Genesis 38:8–10). Onan purposely
interrupted intercourse to prevent conception when it was his duty
to provide offspring. While Onan's act was not masturbation, it was
a sex act specifically directed against procreation, and both Onanism
and masturbation in males involves the deposit of semen where
procreation could not occur. The story of Onan was thus cited as a
basis for the position that any sex act without the potential for
procreation is evil and sinful.

While Onanism is not self-stimulation, the issue cannot be
dismissed as having no relevance at all to masturbation. One
interpretation of the biblical condemnation of Onan does relate to
masturbation because it is that any sex act outside the context of
potential procreation is evil and a sin. This would include not only
the withdrawal method of contraception but also any other birth
control method or sex act of a male other than intercourse. The only
logical conclusion for this position is that the only purpose and
acceptable expression of sexuality is for procreation.

Before this century, that position was supported by the limited
scientific knowledge of the time. Semen was understood to be a
powerful life-giving substance since it caused pregnancy. It was felt
that removing it from the body drained away energy and strength.
Therefore, men were told that they should avoid ejaculation unless
the goal was procreation and that this would result in conservation
of semen and, thus, conservation of strength. It was assumed that
there was only a limited supply for a lifetime and once that supply
was used up it was gone. The fact is, of course, that sperm and
semen are produced regularly for the lifetime of most men and one
way or the other are regularly released from the body.

It is not surprising that this incorrect reasoning led to the belief
that healthy, robust, strong young men were that way because they

did not masturbate and "waste" their semen. Conversely, the sickly, pale, thin, weak boy was that way because he habitually drained this life-giving force from his body. It is a pity that many young men stricken with infectious diseases or malnutrition were condemned and stigmatized with such accusations.

Incorrect speculations continued until this century when hormones and bacterial infections were understood. Because the physical changes of puberty were not known to be caused by hormones and because semen first appeared as pubertal changes occurred, it was assumed that it was the vital energy in semen that caused the development of the genitals, pubic hair, the beard, and muscles. There were theories that if semen was retained in the body the most potent parts of it reentered the blood and produced not only the physical changes of puberty but also the remarkable physical strength and stamina that accompanies male puberty.

A vast folklore developed about causes and effects of masturbation. Substances which supposedly led to this behavior included tea, coffee, tobacco, alcohol, candy, spices, and seasoning while whole grain foods fostered self-control. The habit was disclosed by such varied things as bed-wetting, poor posture, shyness, nail-biting, and cold, sweaty hands. Maladies which it caused were said to include acne, seizures, insanity, and tuberculosis. If a man who masturbated fathered a child, it was said to be sickly and likely to die in infancy. If the child lived, he was expected to not only inherit the habit but also to become insane, a criminal, or both. Imagine the guilt if a father had a stillborn, sickly, mentally ill, or delinquent child.

Current Views

Today it is clear that there is no basis for any belief that emission of semen after any kind of stimulation or nocturnal emission causes any drain of the body's energy sources. This would be a ridiculous deduction from the evidence of modern biology. Both sperm and semen are produced throughout the adult life of a healthy male. In fact, in situations in which energy needs to be conserved—such as starvation or severe illness—male hormone production, semen production, and sex drive all decrease as if the body has its own innate energy conservation mechanisms.

The Roman Catholic church has traditionally held that since procreation is the sole purpose of sex, masturbation is a sin. More recent church statements call for a more positive, understanding approach but still consider it a grave moral disorder resulting from profound problems. Some Protestants consider it a sin; others say it is a sin, but not a heinous one. Still others consider it either less than ideal behavior or normal behavior that might not be avoidable. Most commonly, religious discussions of masturbation are vague and leave a teenager feeling that he is weak and lacking self-control if he masturbates.

All studies of human sexual behavior agree that most people masturbate at some time in their lives. Most of those who try to abstain because they feel guilty fail. There is no scientific evidence that masturbation causes physical or mental harm. While this is true, it is also true that harm may result from guilt or anxiety associated with masturbation.

The question of masturbation is a complex one that should be examined in light of all available knowledge. It requires an individual decision as with premarital intercourse. It may be more of a problem in modern society, since these days people generally do not marry for ten or more years after reaching sexual maturity. In previous centuries, sexual maturity occurred at a later age and was soon followed by marriage. God created humans with an interest or drive to have sex almost anytime in contrast to most animals who are interested only during breeding season. This sex drive is a fact throughout life.

Experience and Behavior

As we saw in chapter 3, various surveys report that about 90 percent of all males masturbate. For females, the figures range around 70 percent. Although most adults today consider it a normal part of life or a normal way of release, some indicate that they find it depressing and some feel guilty. Most males hear about masturbation from others before they experience it, while self-discovery is more common among females.

Most teenagers are very private about their sexual thoughts and experience and may not share them with anyone. Males are more likely to share the newly discovered phenomenon with other boys of similar age, even brothers. If a prepubertal child learns about masturbation, he may try it. Because both males and females are capable of orgasm before puberty, they may experience that, too. A young male may experience orgasm before he is able to ejaculate. Rarely does this become a habit before puberty however.

Because many youngsters learn by self-discovery, they are unaware that masturbation may lead to orgasm. The mounting pressure from the stimulation may lead to a climax that is both shocking and surprising. In males, the ejection of semen may be even more shocking and at first they may think that they've harmed themselves. But because the experience results in such a pleasurable sensation, the act is likely to be repeated.

Although 75 percent of all males experience their first orgasm as the result of masturbation, some may experience their first ejaculation and orgasm during sleep as a nocturnal emission or wet dream. This may not happen until after considerable pubertal development.

Why, when, and how masturbation occurs varies. Some do it for its pleasurable feelings, some to relieve sexual tension, alleviate loneliness, or to get to sleep at night. Sometimes it is simply a habit.

While fantasy is common during masturbation, it is not universal. Some simply concentrate on the feeling, some on getting it over with before being discovered. About 20 percent of males and 40 percent of females who indicate that they masturbate say it is never associated with fantasy. But 65 percent of males and 50 percent of females always fantasize during masturbation. Some read sexually stimulating material or look at pornographic pictures. Most of the time fantasy is about heterosexual activities. Some concentrate on thoughts of other people having intercourse; such fantasy is interpreted as trying to avoid the sin of committing immoral sex acts in the mind. Fantasy during masturbation is obviously a major consideration when deciding on the acceptability of masturbation.

Generally, young Christians report less masturbation than non-Christians, and those Christians who do masturbate report more feelings of guilt and shame. Masturbation is probably the first thought that comes to the minds of many teenagers when they are challenged to commit their lives to Christ and renounce any areas of life they have reserved for themselves. Some teens pray for their sexual desire to be taken away—an inappropriate prayer that is contrary to the way God created us.

The Issue of Acceptability

Making a list of reasons why masturbation is or is not acceptable does not help settle the issue. The perspective that sexuality is God-given and not for the sole purpose of procreation is helpful. The concept of wasting semen doesn't make sense since males produce sperm and semen regularly from puberty on, and, even in the man who has produced numerous children, only a tiny fraction is used for reproduction. But the argument that masturbation is okay because of the need to get rid of accumulated semen is also unfounded. The body has mechanisms to take care of that; semen can simply overflow while asleep or into the urine. In fact the frequency of nocturnal emissions (wet dreams) is more related to subconscious sexual thoughts than to the buildup of seminal fluid. The urge to masturbate is not simply because of this accumulation.

To suggest that masturbation is okay for the purpose of self-control while denying that it involves pleasure is unrealistic. It's like pretending we eat for nutrition only, without sensing the taste. At best, of course, masturbation decreases sexual desire for only a short time, and trying to divert energies through physical work, athletic endeavors, and so on usually doesn't help control it either. This is why most people have concluded that masturbation is a normal release and may be almost necessary at times.

Pointing out that the Bible does not specifically address the subject (which it does not) doesn't help, either. However, there are biblical guidelines that indicate how man should love God, treat his fellowman, and think about himself.

All Christians would agree that marriage is the proper place for the expression of sexual feelings, but not all will agree with the next step of reasoning. If sex is given to us as a means of communion with our spouses, masturbation before marriage or during a separation does not necessarily abuse or decrease the significance of marriage. It certainly would if the spouse were available for intercourse, however.

Masturbation does not necessarily defile the body any more than eating does. Inappropriate gluttony or inappropriate masturbation are both defiling, but eating per se is not always inappropriate. If masturbation does not defile the body or imply sexual immorality, and if we agree that sexual pleasure is not a sin in itself, masturbation is not necessarily a sin. There are important qualifications to this statement though.

Masturbation is wrong if it involves committing immoral acts in your thoughts—lusting itself is sinful. If masturbation involves thoughts that dehumanize others, it is wrong. It is also wrong if it becomes an uncontrollable habit or is associated with guilt, feelings of inferiority, or self-dislike.

Masturbation before marriage may be considered acceptable to many who consider it part of God's gift of sexuality. As with the rest of living, if self-control is the guideline, man can be a sensual being with a clear conscience.

Therefore, prepare your minds . . . be self-controlled; set your hope fully on the grace to be given you when Jesus Christ is revealed. As obedient children, do not conform to the evil desires you had when you lived in ignorance. But just as he who called you is holy, so be holy in all you do; for it is written: "Be holy, because I am holy."

1 Peter 1:13–16

5

Homosexuality

Homosexuality is a subject parents need to address for several reasons. First, there is a Christian position on homosexuality that must be explained to your teenagers. You also want to explain the dangers of AIDS and other sexually transmitted diseases to them. At the same time, teenagers need to know that there is a place in everyone's life for deep, satisfying friendships with people of the same sex—friendships that must be differentiated from homosexuality. Last, a teenager needs to know what his or her occasional thoughts, dreams, and actions concerning those of the same sex really mean. It is appropriate for any teenager to read this chapter. Some have persistent or recurrent concerns about their own tendencies. Some, especially some males, avoid developing close friendships with other males because they fear they'll be suspected of being gay or because they receive the message that males should be emotionally independent and self-sufficient. Whether or not teenagers have any of those concerns, reading about these issues can help them understand human sexuality in general or in people they know whom they might be able to help.

Definitions

A homosexual act is a sex act with another person of the same sex. However, every person who has ever participated in a sex act with another person of the same sex is not a homosexual. A homosexual person is one whose erotic choice for sexual activity is with another of the same sex. The choice of a person's sexual partner is not always that firm. For example, when men are isolated together but separate from women, there is an increased amount of homosexual activity. This has been found to be true in boarding schools, military bases, prisons, and work camps. Most of those men, if given the choice, would choose women as sexual partners. Therefore, when thinking about this, it is important to realize that when sexual urges are not restrained, many are willing to take whatever they can find.

A person should be considered a homosexual then only if it is obvious that his or her choice of sex object is another of the same sex. This is apparent early in life for some homosexual persons but not for all. Because gender identity is learned and the object of erotic attraction is often not self-apparent until the age of puberty, many factors can influence young people either toward or away from homosexual attraction. This of course is a dilemma in the counseling of young people bothered by the attractions they feel. To tell a person that he is homosexual and he might as well face it when he really has not yet developed a clear direction could be pushing him into a life that he does not want and could avoid. But, to lead him to believe that he isn't a homosexual when his gender identity is already established in that direction is a terrible thing to do to him.

Homosexual Acts

As parents, you need to remind yourselves that your children are going to wonder, when they first hear about gays or lesbians, what homosexuals do. This is probably especially true for the child who has learned how parts of males and females are specifically designed to fit together. This can be a question that is difficult to discuss in print without being offensive. In general it is fair to say that fondling of all parts of the body are involved. Because of basic differences in male and female sexual response, the purpose of the stimulation is usually more clearly focused in males to lead to an orgasm. This can be attained in a variety of ways, some of them being the same ones involved in foreplay in heterosexual activity. For both male and female homosexual acts, rhythmic pressure is usually involved. One partner often takes a dominant and the other a receptive role, comparable to the traditional male or female roles. It is clear that the difference in the sexual response is not a biological difference but a psychological or emotional one.

The Christian Response

The issue of homosexuality is a very complex one, but there are biblical guidelines on the subject that you should pass on to your children. The Bible speaks strongly against homosexual acts, and homosexual behavior clearly causes people to fall short of the fulfilling lives they are called to live for God, others, and themselves.

Self-righteousness often makes people forget that in some ways we all fall short and fail to live according to our ideals. Because of this homosexuals have historically been subject to unfair prejudices, discrimination, and antagonism. But even though the homosexual's civil rights should be protected, that does not mean homosexual behavior is acceptable for the Christian or above moral judgment. Tolerance within the law is not the same thing as approval—a distinction that teenagers should be able to understand.

As with so many areas of life, a Christian must walk a fine line with regard to homosexuality. He must have compassion for the homosexual. It's wrong to blame people for something they cannot be responsible for, and it's clear that not all homosexuals are responsible for their sexual orientation. Not all males are attracted to females; not all females are attracted to males. No one should condemn anyone for such a tendency, any more than he should blame a man with one leg because he cannot run. But because the practice of homosexuality harms society, a teenager should be taught that a Christian must oppose the practice of homosexuality. The Christian teenager needs to recognize that such behavior exists and should not be tempted to deny a homosexual his or her human rights. He also needs to be free of apprehensions, fears, and anxieties about his own sexuality, realizing that to a large extent, for most at least, sexual orientation is learned, reinforced, and with some can be relearned with motivation and support. He must learn to respect the powerful force that comprises homosexual behavior and not approve of such behavior in himself or anyone else. All sexual behavior should be guided by the same moral guidelines.

One can love a person while disapproving of what he does. Indeed, the homosexual who wants to can alter his actions, and the Christian who dares to become close to that person can help him. That is clearly what we as Christian individuals and a Christian community should do. Because homosexuality cannot be condoned in a person committed to the higher calling of Christ, one should call on God's sustaining power to help him refrain from such behavior, just as we all do lest we fail. If a homosexual is capable of controlling his actions, there is no reason he can't be part of the Christian community; others in the community don't even need to know of his sexual preference.

Same-Sex Friendships

The topic of homosexuality stirs emotions and mixed feelings in everyone, especially since most people occasionally struggle with or doubt their own sexual identity sometime in life, usually during the preteen or teenage years. It is one thing to think about and discuss an admitted homosexual; it is quite different for a young person to consider his own sexual thoughts involving others of the same sex.

Homosexuality is defined as sexual desire for another person of the same sex or actual sexual activity with another person of the same sex. Overt homosexuality is clearly more common among males than females, and so is the problem of conflicting sexual urges that result in the suspicion, anxiety, or fear that one has homosexual tendencies or is, really deep down, a homosexual. This may be related to the more deeply felt and pervasive sexual drive of young males.

Children may participate in sex play with others of either sex, and teenagers, particularly boys, may engage in mutual masturbation or masturbate in the presence of other boys. It is worth noting that the biblical references to all sexual behavior—including homosexual behavior—refer to adults, not children. Sex play among younger same-sex individuals may be a part of normal development and does not need to be considered homosexuality.

Nevertheless, such experiences may leave a young person wondering whether he could be a latent homosexual. This problem, which is more common in males but also occurs in females, needs to be specifically addressed by parents. While all people have sexual thoughts involving others of the same sex to some degree, there is a clear spectrum of these thoughts that ranges from sexual thoughts to fantasy to lust to actions. These thoughts may begin with or simply be a recognition of another's physical attractiveness. Or they may be a legitimate part of the emotions of a developing friendship, involving a friendship's normal love and caring. Such attraction, although it may in one sense be sexual, is different from homosexuality.

Feeling emotions that cannot be distinguished from sexual arousal is not uncommon in situations where there is strong affection, admiration, and closeness between people of the same sex. It is not unusual as part of a developing friendship or during those tender, priceless moments between a young man or woman and an esteemed aunt, uncle, teacher, or mentor. Such attraction, while it cannot be considered totally nonsexual, is not the same as homosexuality, and teenagers should be reassured about this.

These emotions are strong and meaningful. They need to be recognized and understood. They should not be interpreted as unnatural and certainly are not a step toward homosexuality. Such feelings should not result in the fear of expressing the beautiful love of friendship, and fear of physical intimacy is unnecessary in these situations. When such feelings are interpreted as sexual, they must be checked, but recognizing oneself as a sexual being should result in confidence that does not inhibit the development of close friendships with members of the same sex. This type of inhibition is especially troublesome for boys, who need the bonding of male friendships in their lives but are afraid of what other teenagers will say about them. Men and boys should not allow themselves to be bullied out of these friendships by their peers.

Factors Related to Homosexuality

What makes an individual a homosexual? Obviously there are complex factors involved. Teenagers should be told that homosexuality is not caused by any single predominating factor such as genetic inheritance, biological differences, hormone levels, or genital development. Neither is it due solely to early sexual experiences with others of the same sex who are the same age—or even with adults—because most people who have such experiences do not develop overt homosexuality. Multiple factors combine to determine one's choice of an erotic or sexual love object, but it is not clear what the compelling factors are.

You should tell your children, siblings, or friends that if a person fears his or her orientation is homosexual, that fear does not necessarily make the person a homosexual. These fears are very common during adolescence. This is because it is an age of heightened sexual drive and a time of increased discovery. Most who wonder about their tendencies eventually realize or develop their erotic interests in the opposite sex. They recognize that their interest in the libidos or bodies of others of their own sex can be merely a part of competitive comparison that plagues human nature.

But the sexual stimulation from the same sex is all too obvious for other people. They know all too well that nudity triggers a clear desire. Even this, however, does not mean that that boy or girl is destined to a lifetime of homosexuality. Boys who have been victims of sexual abuse and whose homosexual encounters have left them drawn to males have been able to change their erotic attraction. But of course the other side of the story that both parents and counselors have to face is that some people are homosexual. That has to be faced; to tell a homosexual person that he is not only causes him anguish but also reduces the chances of helping him.

Parental Influence

It is clear that a child's sexual identity is not established at birth. Sexual identity becomes established through the expectations of and relationship to role models, particularly parents. This is known from experience with children who are born with genital defects and because of that are assigned a sex that varies from their chromosomal and gonadal sex. While firm scientific data are not available, it is evident that the input from parents is critical. This doesn't mean that a homosexual parent will raise homosexual children. That's usually not true. It means that messages are continually passing from parent to child which build the child's self-image as a male or female sexual being and teach the child how to relate to other sexual beings.

Lack of parental interaction may contribute to eventual homosexuality. This seems particularly true if a boy exhibits excessive feminine behavior and his parent does not discuss the issue directly or indirectly with him and provide appropriate counseling. Evidence suggests that it is not the feminine behavior itself that correlates with an eventual homosexual orientation, but the lack of appropriate parental response to that behavior.

For example, in one instance a young boy clearly preferred female roles, avoided physically competitive activities, and did not like athletics. After careful counseling, it became obvious that this boy had not yet developed any abnormal gender identity. He simply was not comfortable with the common rough-and-tumble activity that he saw as characteristic of males. He honestly felt that girls had it easier and that it was tough to deal with the demands placed on boys. There was no evidence that there was anything sexual about his thinking or about the compulsion he felt to enjoy female roles. When such problems are recognized early and counseling is appropriate, the limited results available so far suggest that such males will not become homosexual. On the other hand, lack of response by parents to the warnings of such behavior is a common story in the past of homosexuals.

Self-Concept

Obviously, self-concept in general and specifically about sexuality is continuously molded by all interpersonal relationships. Generally those occurring at a young age are the most influential. Adult sexual behavior, whether homosexual or heterosexual, is a result of learned or conditioned early-life impressions and feelings about oneself and relationships to others. This may all add up to conditioning that leads to homosexuality through the progressive realization of sexual preference. At any rate because sexual orientation and preference are not fixed at birth, homosexual preference is mainly the product of human relationships during the early years of life.

Just as importantly, throughout life we learn how to love others and whom to love in what way. We love some people because of admiration, benevolence, and common interests. Others are loved for these reasons but also because of a physical attraction that may extend to sexual thoughts and desires.

The problem of the homosexual may not be specifically one of sexuality. It may relate more to a lack of full, true, and wholesome self-love—an inappropriate or unsuitable self-concept or self-identity that involves the incapacity to love others in a nonerotic or nonsexual way. This inability to love in a nonsexual or nonerotic relationship may be close to the heart of the homosexual's problem. Out of this incapacity may develop sexual eroticism without a committed love relationship. For those with homosexual orientation, this problem involves others of the same sex, but it is also a problem for heterosexuals.

The fact that we all continually learn how to love and whom to love provides a basis for encouraging people to change from homosexuality to heterosexuality, because it suggests that such change is possible. It's true that people have changed their sexual orientation, some with God's help and others on their own. Probably the younger the person is, the more likely he is to change.

Conditioning

Speaking more practically, there are several characteristics that may reflect the conditioning which directs people toward homosexuality. One of these characteristics is never learning to relate to those of the opposite sex. Every such statement must be qualified because of the complex factors involved; every boy who doesn't relate to girls as a youth does not become a homosexual. Nearly

61

everyone goes through a stage when he or she doesn't relate well to peers of the opposite sex, but sooner or later we learn to relate, become well-adjusted, and live the full life that God intended for us. Others force themselves to interact with the opposite sex and eventually become comfortable with the beauty of such relationships.

Another rare situation is exemplified by a man who dates the best-looking girls but at the same time tries to create situations where he can see and compare the size of his erect penis with those of other males because of his belief that his penis is smaller than that of the average man. If he cannot accept this fact or envision himself relating sexually to a girl, he may eventually decide he is a homosexual and live as one.

There are also instances of socially withdrawn males who never develop any close interpersonal relationships with age peers of either sex. Convinced they could never attract or become close to a woman, their sexual imagery and fantasies involve other males. They slip into homosexuality as the only way out they can see.

This whole discussion has not been an attempt to pinpoint the causes of homosexuality, but to point out certain factors that feed into the overall conditioning that may channel people toward this orientation. Such factors do not necessarily predict a homosexual destiny. Generally no teenager wants to become a homosexual. Many who do, feel so progressively and inescapably drawn to it that it seems the only alternative is to admit to themselves that they are homosexuals. By the grace of God we know this just doesn't always have to be so!

Practical Suggestions

During late childhood or the early teenage years some sort of sexual interaction with one or more other people of the same sex might occur but this does not mean these people are on their way to becoming homosexual. Sexual interest, which increases so dramatically during puberty, is a response to physical development and sexual desire. The direction of sexual desire is largely learned. This means that a male learns to be erotically attracted to females and vice versa. Sometimes this is obvious from a young age but many are still learning during puberty. Because they still are learning, they are subject to the powerful influences that explicit sexuality brings. Interacting with older males and pornography, particularly videos or movies, are particularly powerful influences. Even when the influence is not overtly sexual, particular objects or body parts may cause arousal. For example, a boy may become fascinated by seeing male feet or biceps. Such allure can become attractive and powerful. These fantasies, for some, are part of the process of a teen's development and identification of sexual preference. Such may or may not eventually lead to homosexual identity as an adult. Whether it does or not, depends, for most, on conditioning.

There are bound to be instances of embarrassment of a sexual cause. For example, the mortification of a teen who develops a semi-erection in the locker room while the other males look on. In the long run, those situations are not harmful and everyone probably has had embarrassing moments with sexual implications. The harm comes if, while a person is still in the process of developing sexual preference, he or she is approached subtly or not so subtly by someone seeking a sexual encounter. We shouldn't be naive; we need to realize that this may happen, even in churches or at church camps. Young people must be made aware that such things happen and be prepared for sexual advances even in settings where it would be least expected. Sometimes the perpetrators of these encounters do not plan them but become trapped in the web of their own sexual preoccupations.

Examples are sad. A camp counselor insisted that his boys shower daily and watched them to be sure. He was indulging his fascination with their genitals. Eventually he fondled some of them. Another summer camp counselor insisted that boys drop their pants and bend over for punishment. The boys noticed that he developed an erection each time he did this.

The most serious problems result when one boy is picked out by an older male. Situations are manipulated so the boy is trapped in a position in which he is nearly helpless to avoid a sexual encounter. To the observer, it looks like a wholesome big brother relationship. Big brother may be a respected adult. The interaction begins with harmless conversation and apparently casual physical contact. Then, after waiting for the right moment when no one is around, the older person shocks the victim by reaching for or fondling him.

Parents must prepare their children to avoid this. Your children need to know that you consider physical advances like this inappropriate and that nobody can tell who might be involved. They need to know that you will believe them and want to talk about any suspicions they may have. They need to know that you want to help them if a situation has gone beyond the point of suspicion. As parents we need to believe our children because it compounds the tragedy if they come to us and we react with disbelief.

If the encounter has gone so far that the victim experiences sexual pleasure, even if it is mixed with fear and disgust, he or she needs help. If they recognize a same-sex sexual attraction, most can, with help, retrain their thought processes and develop or redevelop an erotic interest in the opposite sex.

Teenagers commonly wonder whether they have homosexual tendencies. Usually it is part of the learning of gender identity around other sexual beings, both male and female. The more physical the stimulation, the more powerful this tendency may seem. Most children who wonder if they have homosexual tendencies during their teens resolve the question readily on their own. Parents can help even without having to know the embarrassing details. Every teenager should be reassured that homosexual thoughts (tendencies) to varying degrees are a part of being a sexual human. Concern about such a tendency, or even having experienced pleasure from it, does not mean that a person is destined to become a homosexual. If a person voluntarily follows that pathway and reinforces the allure, he may. But everyone has a choice and is responsible for his or her own sexual actions.

64

6

Practical Sexuality

More than half of eighth, ninth, and tenth graders feel that birth control pills protect them from sexually transmitted diseases as well as prevent pregnancy. Two-thirds of boys and half of girls of this age feel it is okay to have sex with someone they've dated for a long time. About one-fifth feel it is okay to have sex with several people. What led them to feel this way? Why are they only partly informed about the facts? As a parent, you need to introduce them to the basic facts and also to interpret for them all of the general things that will shape their values if you don't.

Your children see and hear things every day in songs, in the movies, and on television that would have been shocking twenty years ago and downright unheard of forty years ago. Censorship has become progressively more lax in response to the cry that people should be allowed to form their own opinions. As a result of the revamped standards, stories openly indicate that men are really polygamous, that even if a man tries to be moral he can expect to be unfaithful and adultery is the natural course of things.

Your children also hear vulgar terms for sex acts and body parts and they have to guess or try to figure out what they mean. Without stooping to the level of using these terms, it is certainly appropriate and often important to talk about them, figure out what they mean or imply, and affirm a healthy interest in sexuality in spite of the crude way it is commonly referred to. In our culture, we have to talk to our children about these things.

Although the sexual revolution has mainly led to indulgence without responsibility, it has also forced people to admit their sexuality, which is certainly desirable. People are now allowed to talk about and respond to situations containing sexual messages or implications, while a generation ago, a young person could grow up completely naive about the power of human sexuality. Parents now feel freer to prepare their children for this important part of their lives, and that, in turn, may allow the next generation the freedom to enjoy its sexuality in a responsible manner. After all, you can't guide someone unless you can communicate with him.

No longer can anyone be unaware of human sexual behavior. In the past, the media overlooked sexual indiscretions and were far more circumspect in their coverage of these things, but no more. Public reaction may be one of tolerance or intolerance, but sexual matters are now in the public domain.

Many people in the last few generations grew up in an environment that was so devoid of any discussion of sexuality that it was common for them to believe that their friends, acquaintances, and relatives were above sexual interest or curiosity. This commonly left many feeling that they were bad or weird, the only ones bothered by such feelings, desires, or questions. Guilt and self-disgust were quite often the natural result of this type of thinking. Young people today are more aware of the sexual activities of others, including all kinds of sex acts in all kinds of relationships. The high school student today, even if he is not personally involved, is not likely to be as naive as he was a few years ago.

This pervasive openness makes it virtually impossible for people to hide their sexuality, even if that is their natural tendency. This openness can become a problem if the meaning of sexual behavior is not discussed with young people. Parents should comment on obviously sexual behavior that they disapprove of, or their lack of comment will be interpreted as approval.

As a parent, you can't be expected to carry the whole burden yourself. When all is said and done, we are responsible for our own behavior. Trust is so important between parents and children, but trust is a two-sided business. Children need to be able to trust that their parents are being open and honest with them. But it is just as important that parents can trust their children. Trust has to be built over time and if something happens to erode it, parents need to go the extra mile and build it again.

Sometimes a lack of parental response may arise from the parent's own unfounded inhibitions. After all, there isn't a magic transformation that takes away all of our own psychological problems just because we become parents.

Touching and caressing should be a part of most caring relationships. It should certainly be part of the marriage relationship outside of lovemaking. Outside of marriage, appropriate touching shows our love and care of others. If we love someone, it is all right to hug him. When we care about someone, a touch can express that love beautifully. All of us—especially the young, the old, and the ill—need to be touched, and we all should learn to touch one another in nonsexual situations, keeping in mind that some people are more comfortable with this form of affection than others.

Of course, there is the danger of the inappropriate touching of children, which must be guarded against. The simplest defense against such exploitation is to discuss this problem openly and honestly with the child. Children know which people can appropriately hug and kiss them, and the discussion should emphasize the fact that only parents, doctors, or nurses have any business touching the private parts of a child and even then, only if it is appropriate. Throughout childhood, parents need to be keenly aware of the fact that there are adults who are child sex offenders. Some move viciously from child to child, leaving them with scars that may last a lifetime. Some act out of their own insanity and the perverted sexual fascination that they have allowed themselves to nurture. They manipulate children by spending enough time with them to gain their trust and confidence, then may begin seemingly harmless touching and caressing. You don't need to frighten your children about this but you do need to know with whom they spend time and where. No well-intentioned adult is going to expect times of privacy with your children.

Another inhibition that has persisted in spite of today's openness about sexuality involves referring to the sexual parts of the body. For years people have avoided the use of personal possessive pronouns or actual names. A man may say his wife has cancer of the breast, not her breast. For years, genitals have been called "private parts." A girl's genitals may not be called anything and never referred to specifically, and a boy may hear his penis referred to as a "thing" or "it." This combination of obtuse references and the implication that an interest in the genitalia is bad causes needless guilt and should be avoided. Use the correct names, and if somebody is surprised by overhearing it, that is his problem.

Petting

We know the importance of touching and caressing those we love, but what message should you give your children about petting with a steady date or fiancé? When does petting progress from showing affection to sexual touching? Fondling, stroking, and caressing can be simple gestures of caring, ways of showing love, or plain and obvious sex acts. This whole subject is not even mentioned in the Bible because in that time, there was no dating and little social or physical contact before marriage.

What is the purpose of petting? Is it to enjoy and get to know each other, to experience sexual pleasure, or to express love and admiration? Petting may become progressive. While it stops short of intercourse, it could go as far as orgasm without intercourse. Much petting—particularly for the male—ends in sexual arousal and frustration. On the other hand, if the arousal leads to orgasm, the step to having intercourse is a short one.

Petting obviously carries the risk of losing control, having sex, and becoming pregnant or catching a sexually transmitted disease. The answer commonly given to youths is to carry contraceptives in case they get carried away. While one could compare this to taking a life preserver in a boat with the intention of using it only in an emergency, the analogy doesn't completely fit. It is a curious fact that young Christians who end up having sex do so without using contraceptives much more often than others. It is almost as if having a condom available makes it a premeditated sin while somehow losing control at the moment is more understandable. Carrying a condom has a different implication than wearing a life jacket; human behavior and motivation are involved. As with any risky activity, it is wise to set personal limits before the situation arises. Just as it is wise for any married person to set clear limits involving spending time alone with an attractive person of the opposite sex, an unmarried person in love should set clear limits about how far petting will be allowed to go. The couple should talk this over, not assume anything about the other person and, if it comes to that point, help each other hold the line.

While there are no biblical absolutes about petting, a teenager should be familiar with the scriptural guidelines concerning the treatment of others, self-control, and the sanctity of the human body. Scripture tells us to honor our loved ones because they are part of the body of Christ, and the ultimate dishonor is to use someone for your own sexual pleasure. One of the fruits of the Spirit is self-control. Self-control and respect are part of love and part of the basis of a Christian's behavior and personality. It's God's will that we be holy, but holiness is not a condition into which we automatically drift; it requires controlling the desires of our basic nature and being re-created with a new godlike and holy nature. This re-creation requires a continual renewal of mind and spirit. As far as sex goes, a holy person treats sexual morality seriously while thanking God for His gift of sexuality.

Human choices are never between pain and no pain; they are between the pain that comes from daring to be the person God wants us to be and the pain that comes from living the way our basic desires would direct.

Sexual Innuendo

How should we teach our children to respond when topics of sexuality arise in a social situation? When they hear a sexual joke, should they laugh and pretend they enjoyed it although they actually found it disgusting? How should they respond to pornography, homosexuality, or conversations and discussions about sex?

It's important to remember that sex is good. Our bodies are good, and we shouldn't let anyone take that away from us. Because of our commitment to Christ, we have set a standard for ourselves and our behavior, and we shouldn't let anyone take that away, either.

Christians are often accused of being sober and dull, of believing that sex is bad and being intolerant of sexual sin. In response to this stigma, we need to convey the message to our children that we do believe in sex and enjoy it. When it is enjoyed at the right time and place, we can find it to be one of life's greatest pleasures. But such a position has to be taken carefully, without compromising our standards.

Humor discusses, expresses, appreciates, and enjoys situations that are paradoxical, incongruous, absurd, or awkward—common occurrences in most of life. Sex is so much a part of life that there are many jokes about it, some of which can easily be appreciated by a Christian, while others can't. Part of deciding what can be enjoyed to the fullest is knowing the implications of certain phrases. This applies not only to humor, but also to other forms of communication, including advertising.

Bumper stickers, buttons, signs, and T-shirts are loaded with phrases carrying double meanings, most of them sexual, some of them funny. Some advertising uses sex to make claims that have no basis in reality, such as, "Milk drinkers make better lovers." Other ads play on double meanings, such as the sign in front of a hotel restaurant that reads, "Have your next affair here."

How does a Christian respond to the use of these phrases? First, it's necessary to understand the connotation and implication of the words being used. Discuss those connotations with your children. Second, it's inappropriate to approve of anything that would imply you endorse sexual immorality. It's one thing to recognize the universality of sexual interest and behavior but quite another to do anything that could be misinterpreted by your children or anyone else. If your response is asked for, don't hesitate to be honest. The appeal of sex has been used to sell products and to manipulate people for centuries. We should teach our children to be aware of it, whether it is to coerce us to buy soft drinks, shampoo, or cars. Most claims have no basis whatsoever, so if you drink milk to make yourself a better lover, you have been used for profit of the dairy industry.

Pornography

Because of modern communication advances, more and more people—sadly, even children and young teenagers—are now being exposed to pornography. Many people who would never go into an adult bookstore or theater showing an X-rated movie are curious enough to take home adult movies for private viewing. While the only manipulation involved is the profit motive, the effects of exposure can change sexual outlooks. Teenagers need to be told that explicit depiction of normal erotic activities has a powerful effect on a person. The first viewing is forceful, etching images on the mind that persist and lead to the desire to view more and more. If viewing recurs, it often has an addictive effect. This addicting effect commonly leads to an attraction to depictions that become more bizarre, until they cross the line to viewing acts that are strange, markedly unusual, and clearly distorted, degrading, or violent.

Our response to pornography should stem from its definition. Pornography is intended to cause sexual excitement. Rules of sexual standards can be used to test pornography. Is it dehumanizing to the individuals depicted? If you are married, does it cause you to compare the erotic attractiveness of the person depicted with that of your partner? Does it increase your sexual desire so that you find yourself more often mentally undressing people you happen to see? Most people who have experienced pornography say it does all of these things.

This is an issue that parents and their children ought to discuss if possible. Honest people with a Christian sexual ethic sooner or later choose not to view pornography because it minimizes sex, cheapens and dehumanizes it, and erodes the foundations of the marriage relationship.

Every day of their lives, Christians will meet and interact with people who do not agree with or live by their standards. In each of these instances, the interaction should never rob either person of dignity or the possibility of change. People do learn and change, and the possibility of salvation is there for everyone, no matter how they are living at the moment.

As parents, Christians have the advantage of being able to guide and instruct their children in the proper use of their sexuality from birth. It's a tremendous responsibility, but one of the happiest moments of your life comes when you realize that your children have adopted and are living by the very standards you have been trying to teach them all those years.

7

Alternative to Promiscuity

She had a new man in her life and suddenly her whole attitude about sex changed. Before, she had talked freely about the appeal and attraction of any number of men and her willingness to indulge their sexual cravings. She made it clear that she could and did enjoy the physical gratification of sex as much as any man, although she did draw the line at married men. Then, abruptly, everything changed.

Not only was she no longer interested in casual encounters, she didn't even want to share sexual intimacies with her newfound male friend who had all the qualifications she wanted in a husband. Suddenly—without any feeling of sacrifice—she was willing to postpone her physical pleasure.

This young lady had a glimpse of the reason for fidelity—that the goal of trustworthiness and commitment must involve everything including sex. But a concept of chastity as a virtue just doesn't make sense unless you have a background of biblical values or Greek philosophy. Chastity doesn't make sense to most people in our culture because they don't have this background, but it still makes sense to those whose lives are shaped by biblical values. The support for you or your children while developing or rethinking sexual morals should come from your family and the church. It is wonderful if it does, but it doesn't always.

Is the issue of premarital sex even worth discussing? The majority opinion in today's society is that it's not. With rare exceptions, unless Christian ethics are the basis, only those with strict childhood influences or deeply instilled inhibitions even talk seriously about limiting sex to marriage. Maybe you are past the influence of public celebrities, but your children probably aren't. Well-known personalities don't even hesitate to make public their sex lives. Affairs are talked about openly, as are one-night conquests. One popular young entertainer stated proudly that he lost his virginity at twelve years of age.

Most pastors today have become accustomed to the fact that many couples coming to them to be married are already living together and many more have already been sexually intimate. Sexual behavior of young adults from evangelical churches is not that much different.

If you are a pastor, you probably feel the pressure of this dilemma keenly. You know the problem of seeming judgmental or anti-sex when what you are actually trying to explain is the true freedom that comes from life in Christ.

One of the hardest points to understand about the Christian life involves this freedom that comes through Christ. The seeming contradiction revolves around the fact that true freedom is the result of discipline rather than being a result of the individual's choosing to do whatever he wants. The two types of freedom have entirely different results.

Clearly, this principle applies to our sex lives, too. How it fits with the guidelines provided in Scripture and how it can ultimately lead to the most fulfilling, most free, and most joyful life is the theme of this discussion. The concept is not that God doesn't want us to enjoy life. It's just the opposite: He wants us to, and His guidelines are there to help us. God did not make us sexual beings with the desires and capacity for great sexual pleasure just so we'd have to suppress their expression and be frustrated.

One of the greatest sorrows of our civilization is that of one-parent families, which usually means fatherless families. One-parent families are prominent because so many people today are more than willing to enjoy sex but unwilling to make an unconditional commitment to its consequences. The consequences of sexual behavior can involve more people than the two individuals involved in a given act, and if one allows his behavior to be regulated by his best ultimate goal, rather than by the immediate circumstances, the potential effects of his actions will influence his behavior.

The increase in the percentage of one-parent families in our society cannot be considered without considering today's sexual behavior. Nearly one-quarter of the babies born in America today are born to single mothers, even after the massive reduction in total number of pregnancies through abortion. Sex should not be considered without reference to parenthood. Elton Trueblood reasons that man is more than an animal because he alone realizes that he *is* an animal. This uniqueness extends to the fact that, even though all animals die, only men realize they will die. This reasoning can be applied to sex: Man alone realizes that reproduction results from the sex act. Knowing its biological purpose means that human sexual behavior should be governed by more than the compulsion of a biological urge. Sexual behavior must always be considered in the context of possible parenthood, which implies there should be a willingness to accept responsibility for new lives.

Living together and trial marriage are incompatible with marriage in the Christian context. In fact, identification with such a view probably involves a fundamental misunderstanding of it. Such things are not private matters; the community has a stake in the stability of marriage, and the stability of marriage depends on a trusting commitment that cannot help being affected by reliability and loyalty in sexual conduct.

It's important to keep our thinking straight so we can separate the goals of the best life for each individual and the everyday, practical interactions in which we are Christ's ambassadors. We always need to be acutely aware that even the most committed humans are capable of being holy in thought and deed one moment, then being unrighteous the next.

So while we are building a case for an alternative to promiscuity, we need to think about how we can relate to and encourage those who are living contrary to the life we prize. The clue comes from Christ's interaction with the Samaritan woman at Jacob's well. His example tells us how we should associate with people in this situation. This Samaritan woman had had five husbands and was living with a man to whom she was not married. Knowing this, Christ did not hesitate to associate with her, talk with her, and affirm her dignity. He did not condemn her, but at the same time, He maintained a clear standard. The dilemma for us is to communicate our caring while clinging to our principles of fairness, truth, and justice. The most uncaring thing we can do is to interact with others as if any such behavior were acceptable. On the other hand, shunning or not interacting with those whose actions we cannot condone is equally harmful. Christ said, "Go and sin no more!"

Is There a Right and a Wrong?

One real problem of our culture is disagreement about what is true concerning the basis of our conduct. That basis is the foundation of our society, the basis of our Western culture, and it is too often denied in modern thinking. In spite of what the best minds of the past have concluded, today's assumption is that the problems great minds wrestled with in the past were somehow different or don't apply today. Conclusions made in the past should be examined, not categorically rejected or blindly accepted. The conclusion that there is no certain and objective right independent of our emotions, prejudices, biases, and cravings is naive. Such a conclusion rejects the idea of evil and wrong. This philosophy of self-gratification does not provide any basis for a permanent society. Today's philosophy of the individual's right to sexual pleasure without commitment is too closely related to the high number of fatherless children and of abortions being performed yearly.

The Christian stand, based on biblical principles that Christ taught, must be to state the moral standard clearly and to unequivocally believe in chastity—the limitation of sexual intercourse to the institution of marriage. This does not mean that a Christian commitment results in a lack of desire, but rather in a life of self-control. All people are sexual beings, and usually for most of adult life they can be sexually active while being sexually moral. Indeed, moral people *should* be sexually active, because sex is the most consistently enjoyable physical act in life, designed to be enjoyed.

Because of the implications, consequences, and often assumptions of physical intimacy, it is clear that the Christian way calls for sexual intimacy to be limited to marriage. Sexual intercourse is off limits for the unmarried and for those married to others. That's part of the discipline—not to frustrate us, but so that our marriage commitment to our spouses, our children, other individuals who trust and need us, our community, and the world can be what it is intended to be and what we really desire. It's a matter of trustworthiness.

Because of the very nature of sex, this is clearly the best way to build the foundation for the trusting relationship to which we are committed. Fulfilling that commitment is not easy, and most people don't. It is obvious that any stand for limiting sex to marriage is a voice crying in the wilderness today. If any message of our society is clear, it's that part of the full life to which everyone is entitled all of the time includes freedom of sexual expression. It is implied that this sexual freedom is part of having it all together, enjoying good self-esteem and self-expression.

Some recent surveys suggest that indiscriminate sexual activity has passed its peak. There is a decline in the reported incidence of intercourse among both male and female college students. Whether this represents a true change in trend will become apparent with time, but the overall climate hasn't changed. One recent magazine survey indicates that 66 percent of all men expect to have sex by the third date with a woman and 80 percent expect it by the fifth date. Such figures do not suggest that the general attitude about casual sex is changing.

Chastity, an outmoded word, means moral sexual conduct. It should not be confused with *celibacy*, which implies a lifelong lack of sexual activity. For most people who are intent on following Christ, chastity only means abstention from intercourse until marriage. After marriage, everyone is expected to relish sexual activity with his or her partner.

One can begin discussing the case for chastity by considering what sexual intercourse is or what we would like it to be. Should it be more than the biological union of sexual organs, the pleasant feelings that accompany this, and the temporary satisfaction of a basic biological urge? If so, how can it be more than that, and how can it become everything that it has the potential to be?

Intercourse is either a celebration of total commitment or it isn't. It can't be both. If it begins with no commitment, it is difficult to bring commitment in at a later date. If intercourse occurs before that total commitment, or with others while married, it simply cannot be a celebration of total commitment. This is true in a spiritual and practical sense. If part of a person's life involved sexual escapades, as a fully committed spouse, he has to decide whether or not he will tell his wife about his past. He may decide he cannot be totally honest, or he may be honest and risk the consequences. Either way, at times when he is away from his wife, it would be easier for him to have sex with someone else if this had been his previous pattern. If he has told his wife, this adds a significant strain on her trust.

Casual sex is not the same as sex within a marriage. It's only a fraction of the total sharing available in marriage—spiritual, emotional, intellectual, and physical sharing. Intercourse can and is meant to be the pinnacle, the consummation of completeness in a total relationship. Imagine two mountain climbers who reach the summit after days of struggling together, taking risks, giving to each other, only to see two others being dropped off at the summit by a helicopter. The view and the feeling is the same for both couples, but the meaning is profoundly different.

Paul indicates that if two people have intercourse, they physically become one, but the oneness of marriage is more than physical. Sexual union does not make a marriage. The whole process of leaving, cleaving, and becoming—the process of commitment—is what results in oneness. In this light, there is no question that extramarital sex is a paltry substitute for the joy of sex within marriage.

The Sexual Revolution

A sexual revolution has occurred in our society. While there have always been some sexually promiscuous people in the world, the percentage has greatly increased over the past twenty-five years. Changes in sexual behavior are striking, and these changes involve both sexes—differences for females are actually more dramatic than for males.

Results of surveys among single males and females vary greatly, depending on the region sampled and the cultural and socioeconomic background of those studied. General overall results indicate that by age twenty, 70 to 80 percent of all males have had intercourse. Twenty years ago, less than 40 percent had. The increase for females is more dramatic, with a rise from about 30 percent to between 70 to 80 percent. The age of first intercourse also has dropped three to four years. About 80 percent over the age of twenty are now sexually active. Twenty years ago, it was 50 percent (somewhat less for women). Frequency of sex among single males and females is about twice a week, almost twice as frequent as it was twenty years ago. About 66 percent of both sexes do stay with one partner for a prolonged period of time.

The acceptability of sexual pleasure outside of marriage and its pursuit is an obvious current trend. In considering this, it is important to look at the difference church attendance makes, since this attendance implies a greater likelihood of commitment to Christian ideals. The incidence of ever having intercourse among teenagers who attend church is strikingly less than among those who do not: 45 percent compared to more than 80 percent. Nevertheless, the incidence of change over the past twenty years has increased from about 15 percent of churchgoing teenagers to 45 percent. So while church attendance probably suggests a strong influence on such behavior, the upward trend within the church is comparable to the upward trend in society in general.

This trend has resulted from the minimizing of sex, not its maximizing. The availability of the birth control pill cannot be blamed, since it was available twenty years ago. The blame rests with those who minimized sex, some even going so far as to believe it is no more significant than taking a drink of water when you're thirsty. Asserting the unimportance of sexual actions minimizes the consequences of sex.

If sex is minimized—if intercourse is no more significant than taking a drink of water—then using someone's body for pleasure or getting a girl pregnant is also not important. Public communication, theater, and television have minimized sex through the use of comedy, an approach that changes the rules of the game: If tragedy is denied, one can only laugh at the situation.

The message we are hearing from the mass media is unmistakable: Adultery is fun and funny. Such a message clearly has the power to change values and make acceptable that which would be unacceptable if presented in a serious, direct manner. Television comedies continually base their humor on sexual innuendos, which make up much of our best humor. However, humor can obscure the fine line between wholesomeness and undesirability and make the transition to tolerance for irresponsible sexual activity easy and unnoticed. Comedy is such a powerful tool that it denies the tragedy of the situation. Such denial inevitably shapes behavior, particularly of the young. Real-life issues cannot be helped if they are only addressed through comedy; dignity comes through the recognition of error and tragedy.

The sexual revolution can't be separated from the female revolution—women proving that they can be just as "free," sexually and otherwise, as men. This does not deny a justifiable basis for the women's rights movement, and even the need for it. However, agreeing that women have rights does not mean they should want to obtain the same sexual freedom as males. In this instance, women may already have had the better position. But for more than twenty years, the number of virgins among young adult males and females has progressively declined, until they are now a striking minority.

Has the sexual revolution bottomed out in the last few years? If so, it's because people have begun to see the results of the revolution: herpes, AIDS, damaged family relations, unwed mothers, increasing abortions. Some are beginning to think for themselves instead of blindly following the crowd, and they have come to see that the beauty of sex has been perverted into something ugly.

The Joy of Commitment

While some of the greatest sorrows in life—spoiled human relationships—are connected with sex, some of that which is most beautiful in life is also connected with sex. Sexual intercourse is meant to be more than a physical act. If it is only physical, it is simply an animal act. The Christian life elevates intercourse into communion, an act to be partaken of only with total commitment, turning the act of sex into a symbol—an affirmation of that total commitment. This doesn't mean that every sex act is solemn or that the symbolism is even in our minds, but the communion is still there. The sex act should be both a celebration of commitment and an intensely enjoyable experience, which is not inconsistent with the fact that the act also satisfies a primitive biological urge.

Sex may be the strongest social force in our world. If so, no other commitment is more important than the commitment between marriage partners concerning sexual faithfulness. It is simply unfair to expect your spouse to care for you if you allow yourself to debase her worth by having sex outside of marriage.

While many accept the commitment that rules out sex with others while married, they deny that this applies to intercourse before marriage. There are two types of premarital sex: casual sex, involving little or no affection, and sex with the one you love and intend to marry. Do morals change if the other person is the one you intend to marry? Denying oneself sexual intercourse until after marriage enhances sex. It expresses the ultimate in respect for the loved one and his or her worth. How significant is the culmination of marriage if you have already experienced the most physically intimate and pleasurable act that two people can experience in this life? In a love relationship, sex can't be totally separated from the marriage ceremony. The incentive that comes from a public statement before the people who are most important to you should be a valuable and potent result of that ceremony. Every marriage needs all the help it can get, and the expectations of those important to us become a powerful incentive and force in our lives.

Outside of marriage, the sex act is likely to imply more commitment on the part of one participant than on the part of the other, regardless of what is said in the heat of passion. When consenting to their first act of intercourse, most women believe that their partner is the person they will marry; they perceive the act as a commitment, while the male usually does not.

Because sex is so important to humans, it should begin in a setting that enhances the relationship. It should be the right setting for learning together, because no matter how much one reads about sex, learning to give and receive sexual pleasure is a lifelong process. Even married sex is not necessarily wonderful at first, but with marriage commitment, both partners are assured of time to learn, time to enjoy, time to grow together—something that is not guaranteed in casual sex at all.

What if, as is true of so many today, sexual intimacy has already been experienced by one or both partners? Does this spoil the richness of total commitment in marriage? No, not if, by God's grace, the person is able to change, to seek forgiveness, and accept renewal.

What about those who have grown up in a different culture or in a different subset of our culture? What about those who never had the advantage of a home and parents who were committed to each other? It's simply unfair to expect people from these environments to live according to principles they have never been taught, and we must be willing to be patient while they learn the benefits and joys of commitment. Meanwhile, as Christian parents, we must be sure that our children do learn how we feel about sexual morality and why, what such a life has to offer them, and the rewards that await them in their own committed marriages.

8

Marriage

Most children from stable homes understand the value of a good marriage and the lifetime commitment around which it is built. They don't appreciate all of its joys, but they welcome the warmth and security it provides in their lives, and as they grow older, they appreciate the work that their parents have put into providing them with this type of homelife.

Parents rarely sit their children down and teach them about marriage; the lessons are more or less absorbed through day-to-day observation. But children do have to be reminded that marriage is one of the most important parts of life for most people and the best way to express their sexuality. The material in this chapter will probably be of more interest to your older children, as they anticipate marriage, or to you, as a married person, than to your young children. It should be useful for teenagers to read, and it does contain points that you will want to pass on to children of all ages as the opportunity arises.

Changing Concepts About Marriage

One effect of the sexual revolution has influenced even those who have not physically participated in it: the waning emphasis on marriage. That special institution of mutual commitment between husband and wife simply is not held in much esteem anymore, and this is having a far greater social effect than the fact that people are living together without marrying. It can be argued that a ceremony proclaiming a commitment is unimportant because it does not change the underlying commitment. In one sense this is true, but in fact the significance of the marriage ceremony itself has been changed.

The majority of those who marry now do so without believing that marriage means total commitment. No modern word captures the concept of total commitment—premarital abstention from sexual activity followed by a pledge of lifelong faithfulness—so we use the old word *chastity*. Chastity means refraining from sexual intimacy with anyone but a marriage partner, while elevating sex within that marriage to a special, important place. Chastity implies control of one's impulses and desires. It does not imply innocence, absence of temptation, or abstaining from intercourse within the marriage.

Participating in the marriage ceremony without believing in chastity denies the traditional meaning of the ceremony itself, which historically included a vow of chastity. During this celebration the man was asked, "Wilt thou have this Woman to thy wedded wife, to live together after God's ordinance in the holy estate of Matrimony? Wilt thou love her, comfort her, honor, and keep her in sickness and in health; and, forsaking all others, keep thee only unto her, so long as ye both shall live?"

The meaning of the couple's vow in the traditional marriage ceremony is plain; any sensible person knows what it's talking about. One may object to the old wording, but that does not change the basic pledge.

Modern revisions of the wedding vows have frequently involved a deemphasis or absence of the vow of faithfulness. One couple changed only one word but effectively altered their entire commitment, making their promises valid only "so long as ye both shall *love*." Love, as it is understood today, rarely lasts a lifetime, so the point of this couple's commitment was totally lost by the change of that one word.

Feminists object to the word *obey* in the bride's pledge. It's worth noting that the wording of the woman's pledge in the traditional Protestant ceremony is the same as that of the man's. Contrary to general belief, the word *obey* was not originally there; it was added some revisions later. The pledge from the 1928 *Book of Common Prayer* reads: "I, _____ take thee, _____, to my wedded Wife, to have and to hold from this day forward, for better for worse, for richer for poorer, in sickness and in health, to love and to cherish, till death us do part, according to God's holy ordinance; and thereto I plight thee my troth." The bride's pledge is exactly the same, except that it ends with "thereto I give thee my troth."

Plight means to put or give in pledge. *Troth* comes from the twelfth-century word meaning truth, loyalty, or faithfulness, so the statement is clearly a pledge of total commitment for life.

Updating the wording and not observing the traditions are one thing; changing the meaning of the vow is quite another. The deemphasis or evasion of the pledge of total commitment reduces the significance of the marriage ceremony.

Today's deemphasis on marriage has also placed considerable pressure on religious denominations. Their position is awkward because the Christian stand upholds the high position of marriage. On the other hand, the church needs to respond with compassion to people when they are caught in difficult situations or fail (as we all do) to live up to our best standards.

Divorce is not part of the ideal life, but Christ recognized that it happens. Pressure from society has resulted in most Protestant denominations softening their positions concerning divorced persons, remarriage, and acceptance by the church. While the Roman Catholic church has maintained its stand concerning divorce, the number of annulments it has allowed has increased dramatically. This clearly is a response to the difficult situation of divorced people who want to stay within the church when they remarry. To declare that such a huge number of marriages never existed, however, is astounding. The basis for one annulment was that, after thirty years of apparent marriage and five children, the marriage had never happened because the man was forced into the wedding ceremony by his intended's pregnancy!

Sex in Marriage

Marriage can be the most joyous, fulfilling, and meaningful of all possible relationships. It's the one relationship that has been compared with that of Christ and the body of believers. It is far more than a social and legal contract. Historically, marriage had little to do with sexual attraction. The basis of marriage was primarily practical, with the choice of the spouse being made by the parents. Marriage served as the only socially acceptable way for a man and woman to express their sexuality and have children.

Although we consider such arrangements barbaric today, many of those marriages were successful because they fulfilled the criteria of a true marriage: the keeping of promises, honesty, fairness, unselfishness, and obedience. In fact, these factors are more important to a happy marriage than erotic love, which may involve deceiving a spouse, betraying a friend, and abandoning children.

Today, people are free to choose their own marriage partners. Erotic love should be a part of that choice, but it need not be and often is not the initial compelling force. Meaningful relationships are usually not built exclusively on the basis of sexual desire. They develop from friendship to total involvement in the entire personality of the other person, until the couple decides they want to be together, talk together, share everything, and spend the rest of their lives together. During the growth of this relationship, sexual desire also grows.

But this is quite different than expecting sex by the third date, as two-thirds of adult males do today. There is a difference between wanting your own sensual pleasure and wanting to be totally involved with a beloved person. Love for one particular person results in a desire for the whole person, not just for the pleasure he or she can provide.

At the other end of the spectrum, many people are misinformed about the importance of sex within marriage. They are told that sexual fulfillment should be only a by-product and that the act is something selfish and less than honorable if it is approached solely for personal physical satisfaction. Many have been instructed that their aim should be to satisfy their partners and that it is wrong to seek their own pleasure. This implies that there is something wrong with fulfilling the sexual drive within marriage. In fact, personal sexual desire can be fulfilled without diminishing the receiving and giving of pleasure of the totally committed relationship. The sensual pleasure of married sex cannot be surpassed. The difference is that, when the object of physical sex is one's beloved, even when the urge is the most intense, the partner is still more important than the fulfillment of the physical need.

Sex in marriage allows for the ultimate in physical sexual pleasure. A man does not have to deemphasize his sensual feelings and their gratification to concentrate solely on satisfying his wife. The couple can create time for both to give and receive physical pleasure. Knowing that her husband's sole object during sex is to bring her to climax is not conducive to any woman's sexual enjoyment!

Being a good lover in marriage includes understanding human sexuality and the difference in male and female sexual responses. "Letting nature take its course" does not lead to the fullest, most fulfilling sexual experiences. Both are wise to invest in, read, and reread a good sex manual early and repeatedly in their marriage, so they will know what to expect and how to maximize pleasure for both parties. Such manuals are readily available in Christian or other bookstores. It is important to be careful when reading manuals not written from an approach honoring chastity because practices that could be harmful to the committed couple may be advocated.

Historically, marriage manuals began to become more specific during the 1940s and 1950s. However, when they became more specific, they often included rigid guidelines. For a long time, they wrote that the husband should bring his wife to climax at the same time as his orgasm. Many couples tried and tried to achieve this and never or seldom did, with much frustration. The husband felt guilty about his pleasure and the wife felt there must be something wrong with her. Likewise, books should not list taboos for couples. For example, one book instructed that a husband should stimulate his wife's genitals only with his penis, but never use his hands. This implies that there is something unwholesome about genital caressing. And further, it is well known that less then 30 percent of women can reach orgasm from the stimulation of penile-vaginal movement while most can when other stimulation is provided before or after.

The truth is, the only people who should make any rules about a couple's sexual behavior are the couple themselves. The goal of sex is simply to enjoy the pleasure of this special physical celebration; what happens in the process can and should vary. With time, freedom, and experience, each person in the relationship will become familiar with the responses of the other, and the act itself will become more and more pleasurable for both parties.

Both partners should become familiar and relaxed with the other's body. Each man should know the parts of his wife's genitalia. The clitoris is most likely to be a mystery but as soon as the wife can relax enough, her husband should be able to examine it. Only then can he understand how to be a gentle and considerate lover. Conversely, a wife should be acquainted with her husband's genitals, both when he is relaxed and when sexually excited. This kind of openness certainly doesn't have to occur on the first night; it may take months or even years.

Intercourse should be the complete expression of love, caring, and commitment between a husband and wife, a time of total sharing and communication. At the same time, it satisfies some very basic human urges, so it should be fun and enjoyable for both parties. On some occasions the physical part will seem more important than the closeness; other times it will be just the opposite. Sometimes each partner will be looking for different things in the act, and this is fine, too. Basically, whatever works and is acceptable to both partners is good.

Desire

The sexual response in relation to the sex act can be thought of as phases. The process begins with desire on one or both partners' parts. The desire may be a response to cues or related to thoughts and built-in sex drive. The frequency of sexual wishes and thoughts varies with age, health, and life-style, and of course between the sexes. A common complaint of young men is that they would like to have sex more frequently than their wives would. Men, however, by nature can be turned on instantly while it is usually a slower process for women. Women tend to get interested in intercourse because it involves touching, holding, and hugging. Generally nothing works better in stimulating desire in a wife than gentle touching and talking throughout the day or evening.

Arousal

The first phase of sexual response in relation to intercourse should be desire by both the husband and wife. The phases of sexual response which follow have been termed arousal, the plateau stage, orgasm, and relaxation. There are no set time limits for each stage, and each couple will move through the stages at their own pace, which may vary from act to act. Again, it's best to listen to your own body, observe the reactions of your partner, and do what feels comfortable to you both.

Arousal involves both emotional and physiological responses. The emotional response is a feeling of excitement. The physiological response results in genital changes. The changes in the man, of course, include an erection; in the woman they include vaginal lubrication. The mental and bodily responses are not always the same. A woman may have vaginal lubrication but not feel really sexually excited.

Men often think of foreplay as something they have to get through as fast as possible so they can get to the real thing. This doesn't mean that they are insensitive or brutish. Both the male and female perspectives need to be heard and understood. The strength of male sexual desire is focused on reaching an orgasm. Men are turned on quickly and driven to reach the pinnacle, the sooner the better. They have to remind themselves again and again how important this stage is to their wives. Many couples have discovered, however, that this becomes less and less of a problem over the years. This is because many men discover that they need and want more stimulation to heighten their excitement and attain an erection.

To a man, sex is an act largely separate from the rest of life; to a woman, it is entwined with the total relationship. A wise man learns to court his wife long before bedtime, to show his love and concern for her—as well as his physical attraction to her—to kiss and hug, and to take the garbage out without being asked. This kindles the desire and begins the arousal. This is something that the wife will have to explain to her husband (usually more than once). Although he will eventually catch on, there will be times when he'll just want to forge ahead.

After the decision to have sex has been made, actual foreplay begins. Kissing, embracing, fondling, and petting all play their part in arousing both parties. At this point, the whole body is an erogenous zone—earlobes, the back of the neck, the eyelids—whatever your partner enjoys. Movement of body against body is extremely arousing, no matter what body parts are involved. This is the time for exploration and truly knowing your spouse, and both should feel free to make suggestions about new areas they would like to explore.

The husband will achieve an erection during this phase, perhaps quite early on, but most men learn that ten to twenty more minutes of stimulation is worth it and results in maximizing pleasure from orgasm. The erection may fade and return several times as petting continues while the wife progressively becomes sexually excited. Lubrication of the vagina indicates the beginning of a woman's arousal, but foreplay should continue beyond this point.

The Plateau Stage

This stage is a time of heightened excitement for both parties. The woman's nipples become firm and stand out from the breast. As her excitement builds, her clitoris swells and the major lips at the entrance to the vagina enlarge to two or three times their usual size. Swelling of the lower part of the vagina reduces the diameter of the outer third of the vagina by about 50 percent, allowing it to fit tightly around the penis.

During this phase, the woman will enjoy manual stimulation of the clitoris and the area around it, which is generally necessary for her to experience an orgasm. The husband's actions should be directed by his wife's reactions and should always be gentle. Men enjoy fondling of the genitals, too, including the scrotum and the underside of the penis, which helps maintain an erection. Lubricating fluid may appear at the tip of the penis at this stage. Once the wife's labia minora (the smaller lips on each side of the vaginal opening) swell, she is ready for insertion of the penis, which should be done slowly and gently. Of course, it is not meant that a couple should proceed from stage to stage mechanically. The act will differ from time to time. When the penetration of the penis occurs should be a mutual decision, sometimes earlier and sometimes later.

Intercourse

The actual act of intercourse begins with the man thrusting his hips to push his penis into his wife's vagina or by the woman lowering her vagina onto her husband's penis. Positions of intercourse are variations of a few basic ones: male-above, female-above, lateral, and male-behind. There are many variations of each of these. The most common position is the male-above. It gives the man freedom to move and control his thrusting. The wife lies on her back with her legs comfortably spread, the man above, supporting most of his weight on his arms and elbows. Usually his legs are inside hers but during the act the couple may shift, for example, after entry she may close her legs.

In the female-above position, the husband lies on his back with his wife straddling him from above. She inserts the penis and then moves back on it and controls the timing and depth of penetration, leaving the man's hands free to continue stimulating her. The lateral or side-by-side positions may begin as such or as a male- or female-above with turning or rolling later. Because neither partner has weight to support, arms are free for embracing. The male-behind (rear entry) positions are also several. Penetration is from behind. The most common objection to this position is the lack of face-to-face contact. This position leaves the husband's hands free for caressing and is sometimes used in late pregnancy, since it puts no pressure on the woman's abdomen.

During intercourse, a couple may change positions as often as they want. How often they change may depend upon how leisurely their lovemaking is. If petting to the point of insertion has been so intense that the urge is to not interrupt, one position will be maintained to build to orgasm. But at other times, variety will be added by shifting position, often without withdrawing the penis. Or the couple may separate and assume several positions during the act. Sometimes they may separate and spend more time stimulating each other in various ways before reuniting. This can be a helpful way to stimulate the woman and bring her to orgasm.

Orgasm

Sexual tension builds in both partners as the thrusting continues. The climax is reached and experienced as an intense, pleasurable feeling. This is accompanied in the man by the ejaculation of semen in a series of quick spurts. Sometimes simultaneous orgasm is possible for man and woman but usually not. Because of basic male-female differences, while it usually takes a woman longer to attain sexual excitement, she may at times be able to experience one or more orgasms but at other times feel that having one every time is not necessary. So she may be satisfied with the tenderness, closeness, touching, and feeling without an orgasm, while her husband seldom will.

The aim of each act of intercourse is to bring satisfaction to both partners. A husband may do this by rhythmic stimulation before penetration, trying to achieve penetration without breaking the rhythm, and continuing until he brings his wife to orgasm. Both may rely upon the rhythmic genital friction to bring them to climax. Quite often the man's orgasm comes first, but he can and should still bring his wife to orgasm through continued caressing of the clitoral area, if she wants.

No other physical experience involves the intense sensations of excitement and release that orgasm does. It has been described as beginning with a momentary feeling of suspension, then an intense feeling is centered in the pelvic region in both males and females. But muscle and nerves throughout the whole body are involved and the sensation of intense pleasure reaches the whole body.

In both males and females, orgasm involves a series of rhythmic contractions of muscles of the genital-reproductive structures and the pelvis. In the woman this involves rhythmic contractions of the lower third of the vagina. Intense emotional sensations accompany these contractions. In men, the contractions first move seminal fluid and sperm into the prostate gland and then into the urethra. The muscle contractions rhythmically ejaculate the semen out the end of the urethra. When the first contractions start to move the semen into the prostate gland, men sense that ejaculation is inevitable.

Relaxation

The last phase of the sexual response should include a sense of satisfaction. The natural resolution is very different for men and women. A man's penis rapidly decreases in size. He is very relaxed and it is a common tendency to want to turn over and go to sleep. The genitals of women, on the other hand, take fifteen to twenty minutes to return to their unstimulated condition. The excitement also takes longer to subside.

During this phase, it is often important for the wife's sake that the couple continue to enjoy the warmth and closeness of being together. Kissing and hugging may continue for fifteen to twenty minutes before all signs of arousal subside. Sleep may follow: both should be completely relaxed.

The Sexual Christian

A Christian commitment can entirely change a typical person's sexual history, because it provides an impetus for the individual to control his or her biological urges. Whereas a typical young man feels compelled to prove himself by having sex during his teen years, the young Christian is more capable of thinking through his actions and resisting this form of pressure. Courting couples who might otherwise take part in sexual activities are more likely to wait for the total commitment of marriage.

Most people marry sometime during their twenties and will have intercourse frequently during the early years of marriage. Males are generally more likely to want to experiment with different techniques and may be more interested than females in variety in intercourse and foreplay. A young male is generally more quickly aroused and will reach orgasm more rapidly than his spouse, who may not experience as much satisfaction as the male during this time of life.

The natural course of the marriage relationship results in less eroticism after a few years, decreased frequency of intercourse, and sometimes dissatisfaction with the marriage, something that need not be true for the committed couple. Among women, sexual interest peaks between the ages of thirty and fifty, and after menopause, there may actually be an increase of sexual interest. The older man becomes more like the woman, in that he becomes more interested in the total sexual encounter rather than just in intercourse, in part because he needs more stimulation through touching and caressing. So a couple committed to each other will actually become more sexually compatible with time.

Considerably more than half of all men are unfaithful at some time during marriage, with the man who was sexually promiscuous before marriage being more likely to be unfaithful after marriage. In spite of the commonly held belief that men are more likely to be unfaithful during their "midlife crises," unfaithfulness can occur at any age. While age is not the major factor, those more highly educated and those who rarely or never attend church are more likely to be unfaithful. In contrast, women, who generally are less likely to be unfaithful, are more likely to be so between the ages of thirty and forty-five. Unfaithfulness in women rarely occurs early in marriage or among regular church attenders, and it occurs more commonly among those employed full-time outside the home.

While the sexual behavior of the Christian clearly need not and should not be that of the typical person, understanding human sexuality and the sex life of the can be helpful to someone who wants to control and regulate his or her own sex life.

The Marital Relationship

Is there a more honorable state than marriage for most Christians? The answer is no, even though some of the thinking that led to moral attitudes and conduct in the past have implied otherwise.

Some thinkers have implied that marrying is giving in to sexual desire and an admission of weakness, which is simply not true. Marriage is an honorable, lofty state of being.

The wording of Paul's first letter to the Corinthians may be the basis for some confusion on this point. The seventh chapter seems to imply that it is good not to marry or have sexual relations, that those who are married should have sex only when they are otherwise unable to control themselves, and that the weak are the ones who should marry. This chapter is not an exposition or commentary on marriage for the Christian, but a series of points addressed in response to issues raised about marriage in the culture and situation at Corinth.

This does not detract from the chapter's application to us; on the contrary, we can only apply the comments when we understand them. The statement "It is good for a man not to marry" (1 Corinthians 7:1) is given in response to a previously discussed issue. It may have been said to bring balance to the statement that all things are lawful or permissible, in response to those advocating strict self-denial. The statement is followed by a statement saying that each man should have a wife. Paul points out that abstinence within marriage may do more harm than good.

The urgency of the Christian mission at that time and the belief that Christ would return shortly, led Paul to indicate that most people should not change their marital status and that marriage could divert the people's primary concern. Paul, however, indicates that marriage and celibacy are both gifts. The fact that every Christian is called to serve God in one state or the other is clear.

Christ also discussed this issue with His disciples after He was questioned by the Pharisees. When His disciples asked Him if it is better not to marry, Christ said that celibacy was only for those who were especially called to it. The implication is not that celibacy is a better way of life, but rather that it is a special way of life. Most people are called to marriage, which they are expected to enjoy.

Should the fact that there is polygamy in the Old Testament imply that monogamy is not held in a high place in God's eyes? No. While polygamy is not explicitly forbidden in the Bible, it is clear that polygamy was not the usual practice: It included problems and disadvantages. Monogamy clearly is the highest form of marriage—two becoming one. Commitment of one man to one woman is possible only in monogamy.

Marriage can and should be the most exhilarating, ennobling, and fulfilling of human relationships. But if it is to be this, both partners have to be willing to pay the price. Seeking personal happiness and a beautiful relationship are by-products of trying to give happiness to your spouse. This involves time, trust, and emotional energy. The point is not who is the boss? what do I owe her? or what does she owe me? The point is how much am I willing to give? how can I be most fair and loving in each situation? Basic to this is honesty, learning to be truthful and open, even when it hurts, and taking time to communicate. Our natural tendency is to not talk about painful things. When this happens for years, more and more things are never discussed and, without realizing it, couples know less and less about each other's thoughts and desires. Two people drift apart because the most important issues, those that are painful and cause disagreement, are avoided.

Pain and anger are part of every relationship. The best way to keep them to a minimum is to confront them when they come up. Much anger can be avoided by simply not allowing yourself to become upset by trivial issues that really don't matter.

Fairness in marriage involves recognizing and allowing your spouse his or her individuality. The romantic ideal of marriage as a relationship in which both partners share every interest and activity isn't very realistic. Although liking someone naturally leads you to want to be with that person, individual interests vary, and they can easily be pursued without hurting the marriage.

Proper attitudes in marriage involve sharing money and resources. Proper trust involves realizing that there are things that need to be kept private, intimacies that are to be shared only between marriage partners. Marriage means being able to say "I'm sorry" and being able to forgive.

Nothing provides a more stable, reassuring environment than a solid marriage. Any child of divorced parents knows that. A stable marriage is the best, and—starting at any point in time, from any situation—each of us is free to strive for the best.

PART II
Facts of
Sexuality

9

Male Sexual Development

This chapter provides an overview of human male sexual development and is quite explicit so there will be no danger of misunderstanding, which can sometimes occur when facts are glossed over in an attempt to be inoffensive. You as a parent may want to read this chapter before your children do, since you are best qualified to decide whether or not your child is ready for this material. You may want to give your child some idea of what he will find in here, perhaps discussing some of the material either before or after giving him the book. If you decide he should not read it himself yet, you will still find the information in here valuable for answering questions or opening discussions on the subject.

Human sexual development and function is discussed here to help readers understand how human sexual organs are designed to work. Sexuality and our God-given sexual organs are basically good, and an interest in sex is both normal and right. There have certainly been times during this century when the pleasures of sex have been seen as inconsistent with the holy life, and some people still grow up believing that the genitals are something to be ashamed of. In part, this is because no one ever told them otherwise in a frank, open, and loving discussion. Others feel this way because they have picked up the message that sex is a shameful but necessary force of life.

The concept of sexual pleasure being shameful is an ancient one. There is an Old English word, *pudendum*, that refers to the external genitals of either sex and derives from the Latin word meaning literally "that of which one should be ashamed." The same root word can also mean "prudent," however, indicating appropriate bashfulness or modesty instead of shame, and it's difficult to determine how the word *pudendum* was actually used in the Old English. But today it's generally considered prudent to understand how our bodies develop and are meant to be used and clearly nothing about physical anatomy or physiology is shameful.

Embryonic Development

The external genitalia of both males and females develop from the same embryonic genital structures. The initial structure, which develops only a few weeks after conception, is a vague elevation referred to as a genital eminence. By nine weeks after conception, this develops into a prominent midline structure called the genital tubercle. On either side of the tubercle are ridges of tissue called genital folds. Outside of the folds are rounded structures called genital swellings. In the middle, below the genital tubercle, is an opening called the urogenital opening. These basic structures then develop into either male or female genitalia.

The genital tubercle elongates into a penis if the child is to become a male, and the genital folds form the skin around the penis, including the foreskin. The genital swellings grow together to form the scrotum. The urogenital opening does not persist, because tissues grow together over it, forming the urethra, the tube that opens at the end of the penis. This opening, the urethral meatus, is the common opening for both the urinary and reproductive systems. Usually the opening is at the tip of the penis. However, if the tube formation ends too soon, it may be on the underside.

The line of fusion of the genital fold that formed the tube that becomes the urethra on the inside and sheaths the penis with skin on the outside can be seen running along the underside of the penis. It is a line of darker skin that is often a ridgelike thickening before puberty. This line or raphe extends down the middle of the scrotum, marking the line of fusion of the structures that grow together to form the scrotum. After the scrotal sac develops, the testes descend from within the body through canals on either side of the penis. Usually the testes descend shortly before birth.

The Penis

The most obvious male sex organ is the penis. The penis is a very specially designed organ, different from any other part of the body because of its ability to dramatically change size and firmness. It is shaped like a cylinder or tube that hangs down when soft but sticks out and up when hard.

The penis contains the tube through which urine passes and therefore is part of the body's excretory system. Urine is formed in the two kidneys, then flows through two tubes (ureters) to the bladder, where it is stored until it is passed through the urethra and out the opening at the end of the penis.

The penis is also a sexual or reproductive organ. While it is usually soft, it has the remarkable ability to become hard and stiff, which makes sexual functioning possible. The proper name for the state of a stiff, hard penis is an erection.

The penis is able to change size and become erect because it consists of three cylinders made of specially designed tissue and tightly bound together by fibers. This kind of tissue is called erectile or cavernous tissue. These cylinders of erectile tissue contain blood spaces that are capable of widening to trap blood that is pumped into them. An erection occurs when nerve signals widen the openings that let blood flow into the spaces and narrow the openings that allow blood to flow out. As more blood is pumped and trapped into these spaces, more pressure builds up within them, which makes the penis become straighter, longer, and harder. So an erection occurs because of a hydraulic system that allows extra blood into the penis and keeps it there. An erection goes away when the openings allow most of the blood to flow out of the spaces. The pressure drops, and the penis becomes softer and limp.

Impulses from nerves stimulate the penis to get hard when it or other parts of the body are touched, as the result of thinking sexually stimulating thoughts, or sometimes without any physical or mental stimulation at all. The nervous system reflex involves the lower spinal cord, so males with paraplegia from high spinal-cord injuries are usually capable of having erections but sometimes bothered by them at undesirable times.

The nerves also send the message to make the penis hard during certain phases of the sleep cycle that occur every night. It's normal for males to have erections while asleep, most of which are not related to sexually stimulating dreams. This phase of sleep is often close to waking time, so a male's penis is often hard when he wakes up, even though he has not been dreaming or thinking about sex. When a male wakes up with an erection, it should simply be a reminder that he is a normal male and does not mean he is sexually stimulated. It is certainly nothing to be ashamed of. Of course there are times when it can be embarrassing. If a male is sleeping where he could be seen and embarrassed if he had to get up with an erection, it is wise to keep a loose shirt or robe nearby.

Erectile Tissue

Two of the three cylinders in the penis have a purpose different from that of the third. These two parts make up most of the space inside a penis and become the hardest when it is erect, making the erection firm and stiff. A male can feel these parts of his penis when it is erect. These two cylinders attach to the bone in the pelvis, one on each side. Because of the attachment to the bone, and because of the hydraulic system that causes the cylinders to become straight when fully erect, the stiff penis points upward.

An erect penis stands out from the body at an angle somewhere between horizontal and vertical. In most, the angle is between thirty and sixty degrees. In a few, it is almost vertical. The angle tends to be highest just after puberty and gradually becomes lower with age. The attachment of the root of the penis to the bone provides the ability to control the movement of the penis during intercourse through movement of the pelvic bones or hips.

The third cylinder in the penis is in the middle of the underside. It also contains spaces that fill with blood when the penis is erect, but it is made of more elastic, less fibrous tissue, so it feels spongy when pressed. The urethra, a tube that leads from the bladder to the end of the penis, passes through this cylinder. The spongy, flexible tissue allows the fluid containing the sperm, the semen, to pass through the tube and be pumped out of the erect penis.

The spongy cylinder becomes wider at the end of the penis and forms a knob-shaped structure that makes up the tip of the penis. This is called the glans penis. When the penis is erect, the glans enlarges and is often bigger around than the rest of the penis. This glans penis fits over the two main cylinders. The edge of the glans—where it joins the rest of the penis—is called the corona. The corona stands out more from the rest of the penis when it is erect, especially in the circumcised male. The urethra, which passes along the spongy body on the underside, opens at the tip of the glans. This slitlike opening is collapsed unless fluid is passing through it.

There are special types of nerve endings on the surface of the skin of the penis and deeper within the glans. Some are just like those elsewhere on the surface of the body, which provide the sense of touch. In addition to these nerve endings, there are three types of nerves that end in specialized sensitive endings called capsules. One of these types of capsules is not found anywhere else in the body. These capsules are uniquely designed to respond to touch, detect pressure, the amount of pressure, and changes in amount of pressure.

The skin on the penis is also specially designed. There is no hair on the penis, except at its base, and its skin is darker and thinner than most other body skin. Along the main body of the penis, the skin is loosely attached, and the tissue beneath does not contain fat cells, which allows it to move back and forth freely. On the other hand, the skin that covers the glans penis is firmly attached to the tissue under it.

When the penis is formed, before birth, a free fold of skin encloses the glans penis. This fold of skin is called the foreskin or prepuce. The skin on the outside of the fold is just like the skin along the shaft of the penis and much of the body. The skin on the inside of the foreskin is continuous with that covering the glans and is moist and soft, similar to the mucous membranes that line the urethra and the mouth.

Circumcision

Often the foreskin is removed in a minor operation called circumcision. Most males in America and in some other parts of the world are circumcised within the first few days of life. In a newborn baby boy, the foreskin sticks to the glans. If a baby is not circumcised, this adherence decreases and after several months the foreskin can be retracted or pulled back off the glans. An uncircumcised male should retract the foreskin daily and wash completely because of the secretion of the glands on the inside of the foreskin. This secreted substance collects under the foreskin and may irritate it if it is not washed regularly.

The uncircumcised foreskin entirely covers the glans before puberty, but after the penis grows to adult size, it may only partly cover the glans penis. When an uncircumcised adult male has an erect penis, the glans penis sticks out beyond the foreskin, so most or all of it is uncovered. The foreskin will usually fit just behind the corona of the glans of the erect penis.

Varying amounts of the foreskin remain after circumcision. Before puberty, even in the circumcised male, the foreskin may overlap onto the glans. The penises of both uncircumcised and circumcised males are essentially the same when erect, except for the extra skin along the shaft, but the glans penis of the uncircumcised male is much more sensitive to touch because it is usually covered.

The uncircumcised foreskin may become chapped or irritated, especially if it is not washed regularly. Handling of the penis or sexual activity can cause the foreskin to become red, sore, swollen, or irritated. Uncircumcised males, particularly when young and inexperienced, are likely to ejaculate early during intercourse because of the glans's intense sensitivity. But premature ejaculation is common among both circumcised and uncircumcised young men, and there is no evidence of any difference in sexual function or sexual sensation.

Of course, circumcision can be done at any age, so if a boy or man is not circumcised and would prefer to be he can check into having it done. Most males in the United States are circumcised at birth even though there is no medical reason to do so. Those who oppose the procedure say it is an unnecessary surgical risk and expense. Those who favor it say it is easier to keep clean or simply feel it looks better.

Penile Length

There is variation in penis length just as there is with the size of hands, feet, noses, and ears. Of course, all penises grow considerably during puberty. After puberty, the average erect penis is six inches in length. Most men have an erect penile length between five and one-half inches and six and one-half inches, and almost all fall in the range of five to seven inches when erect. The extremes of the normal adult erect penis are about four and one-half inches to seven and two-thirds inches. Measurement of a penis is usually along the top. This measurement will vary depending upon how heavy a man is because the root of the penis is attached to the bone and the thicker the pad of fat between the bone and the skin, the more of the length is obscured.

Apparent size when not erect is not necessarily proportional to erect length. The length of any man's flaccid penis varies greatly from time to time. The most common adult length is between three and four and one-half inches but it may range from less than two inches up to six inches. Because a man's flaccid penis will vary in length from time to time, the flaccid length does not mean much. The male who is thought to have a particularly big penis based on locker-room viewing often has a semi-erect penis that will not lengthen much more when fully erect.

Nothing can be done to make an adult's erect penis any longer; any effort to stretch or enlarge a penis only breaks down the tissues that make an erection firm. However, it is important to realize that sexual ability and enjoyment are definitely not related to penis size. Because size actually is about the same for most men and locker-room comparisons are often misleading, it is best not to try to compare.

The Testes

Below the penis is a sac, pouch, or bag of thin loose skin called the scrotum or scrotal sac. The sac contains muscles that allow the scrotum to hang loose when they are relaxed and, when contracted, pull the scrotum up next to the body under the penis, causing the scrotal skin to fold and wrinkle. Inside, the scrotal sac is divided into two halves, each containing a testis.

The testes, or male reproductive glands, have two functions. First, they produce the male hormone testosterone. Testosterone causes the formation of the penis and scrotum of a male before birth and also causes a boy's body to change into a man's at puberty. This hormone provides a man with strength and stamina as well as his sexual and reproductive abilities. The other function of the testes is to produce sperm, the male reproductive cells that begin to be produced in the testes at puberty and are usually produced for the rest of a man's life.

The testes develop inside the body and normally descend into the scrotum shortly before birth through passageways called inguinal canals that lie below the skin on either side of the base of the penis. When they descend, they bring along the cord structures attached to them. After that, the canal contains this spermatic cord, which suspends the testes within the scrotum. The cord itself has muscles within its wall and contains blood vessels, nerves, and the vas deferens—a very muscular cord that transports sperm from the testes.

In a boy the spermatic cord may shorten and pull the testes up to the opening or inside the canals on either side of the penis when he is excited, frightened, or cold, but when the muscles in the spermatic cord are relaxed, the testes hang freely within the scrotal sac. After puberty, the testes are too large to rise as far but muscular reflexes frequently raise and lower the testes in the sac.

The opening from the canal into the abdominal cavity normally closes around the spermatic cord after the testes descend. If this inner opening of the canal or other tissues along the top of the canal develop an opening that could allow the abdominal contents to protrude, this is called an inguinal hernia and should be surgically closed.

If one or both of the testes do not descend normally by birth or shortly afterward, the condition is known as cryptorchidism (a term that literally means "hidden testes"). This may happen if the testis has not developed properly, if there is not enough hormonal stimulation, or if some structure is blocking the testis from descending. In order for them to fully develop the ability to produce sperm, both testes should be in the scrotum throughout childhood. If one or both testes do not descend, hormone testing, hormone stimulation, surgery, or all three should be done to determine whether the testis is normal and bring it into the scrotal sac.

If one testis is damaged, the other will produce enough male hormone at puberty to ensure full male development, and although fewer sperm are produced, the man is usually capable of fathering children. If neither testis develops, hormones have to be given to produce puberty and maintain males as normal adults. Of course, there is no sperm production, so these men cannot father children, but they become fully developed men and are capable of normal sexual function, including ejaculation and orgasm. If a testis has been cryptorchid, or its development was otherwise affected, it may be smaller than the opposite testis. In such cases, the opposite testis may enlarge to compensate for the poorly developed testis. Otherwise, both testes are the same size.

If one or both testes are missing, prosthetic or artificial testes can be placed in the scrotum which are normal in size, shape, and consistency. Of course, such a testis is only for the sake of appearance and does not function.

The testes move up and down freely, pulled by the muscles in the wall of the spermatic cord. Testes elevate in response to touch, cold, and sexual excitement, especially as ejaculation approaches. The testes are also pulled up as the muscles in the wall of the scrotum contract. In the relaxed position, the testes usually do not hang at the same level because of a difference in the length of the spermatic cord and blood vessels. In most men, the left testis hangs lower than the right. This difference in level is important because if they both hung at the same level, they would be more likely to hit together rather than slide past each other when walking, running, or sitting down.

Testes can be damaged if the spermatic cord gets twisted (torsion). When this happens, there is pain and swelling of the testes, and it must be treated quickly by surgery. Any acute pain which develops suddenly in a testis should be examined by a doctor immediately.

A male should learn to periodically examine his testes from puberty onward. Only rarely do testicular tumors develop, but they can be recognized early because of a hardness or irregularity in the surface of the testes. There are other structures in the scrotal sac besides the testes but the testis itself has a smooth surface. Each male should become familiar with his own testes and examine them periodically, perhaps when showering. If he has any questions, he should see his doctor or a urologist.

Other Structures

Each side of the scrotum also contains an epididymis, which is connected along a side of the testis by many tiny tubules. Sperm pass from the testes to the epididymis, where they remain for several weeks and mature. They then pass up the vas deferens (the sperm duct within the spermatic cord) and into the body. The end of each vas deferens widens and forms another storage area, the ampulla, where the mature sperm stay until they are pumped out of the body (ejaculated).

Fluid is added to the sperm from two other types of glands. First is a pair of seminal vesicles, one attached to the end of each vas deferens. The fluid that is produced in the seminal vesicles joins with the sperm when it is ejaculated. The second gland is the prostate gland, which adds most of the fluid to the ejaculated mixture. This fluid, which is a mixture of sperm and secretions from the seminal vesicles and the prostate, is called semen.

Ejaculation

The ampulla and seminal vesicles empty into the ejaculatory duct, which empties into the urethra within the prostate gland. During ejaculation, the muscular tissue of the prostate, as well as the muscular walls of the ducts, rhythmically contract and force the various liquid secretions into the urethra. Contractions of the muscle surrounding the urethra in the base of the penis force the semen out of the end of the penis in several spurts.

An additional set of glands empties into the urethra. During erection and sexual excitement, these glands secrete a clear, viscous, mucuslike liquid that lubricates the urethra in preparation for ejaculation. Drops of this fluid may appear at the urethral opening on the tip of the penis during sexual excitement.

During puberty, the testes enlarge and begin to produce sperm, and the seminal vesicles and prostate begin to produce their secretions. The result is the production of semen. Boys experience ejaculation rather early in puberty, and the first ejaculate usually contains mature sperm. Three-fourths of all boys first ejaculate between the ages of twelve and fourteen; the most common age is late in the thirteenth year. Whether the first ejaculation occurs as a nocturnal emission (commonly called a wet dream), as the result of masturbation or the result of some other stimulation, the mechanism is the same. The stimulation results in impulses that cause the prostate and muscles at the base of the penis to contract rhythmically several times. This results in the series of quick spurts that send the semen through the urethra and out the opening in the tip of the penis. Semen is white, milky, and sticky. The average amount of one ejaculation is between one-half to one teaspoon or less. This amount can vary considerably, depending on the amount of sexual excitement and the frequency of ejaculation.

Usually as ejaculation occurs, it is accompanied by an intense pleasant feeling, a sudden violent, exciting sensation called an orgasm. The desire for this feeling is the basis for much of the male's sexual drive.

Puberty

Puberty is the period of time when the genital or sexual organs mature and the so-called secondary sexual characteristics develop. During this time, individuals become capable of reproduction.

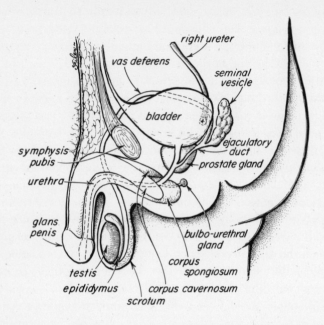

The first change that boys generally notice is the growth of pubic hair. Most boys begin developing pubic hair between the ages of eleven and thirteen. Occasionally a boy with normal development will begin growing pubic hair before or after these ages, some as early as nine, others not until fourteen or fifteen. At least half of all boys first grow pubic hair some time between their twelfth and thirteenth birthdays. Before puberty, boys have some very fine, light hairs around the base of the penis, but pubic hairs are darker, longer, and coarser. At first only one or two hairs grow at the base of the penis or on the scrotum, but they gradually become more numerous over the next several years, until an adult quantity is present. The amount of pubic hair in normal adult males varies considerably. Hair extends onto the scrotum, the abdomen, the thighs, and behind the scrotum.

Although pubic hair is commonly the first pubertal change that is noticed, growth of the testes is actually the first sign of puberty. The testes remain about one-half-inch long from infancy until just before the beginning of puberty, then they gradually enlarge to the adult

110

size of one and one-half to two inches in length. Growth may begin as early as nine. It is usually noticeable between the ages of eleven and twelve, and the testes gradually enlarge over the next three or four years. Any man's testes may vary in size from time to time.

Within six months of the growth of the first pubic hairs, the penis begins to enlarge. It grows in length and width, and prolonged erections become more frequent. The penis usually grows rapidly, with a very noticeable increase in size in a few months, and is close to adult size in about two or three years. In most males, growth of the penis is first noticed between twelve and a half and thirteen, but it may start as early as nine and a half or as late as fifteen. Full development will occur between the ages of thirteen and seventeen.

Body odor, a result of pubertal hormone stimulation, may first develop in early puberty. Many other changes occur in midpuberty—one to two years after genital growth and pubic hair growth are first noted. A boy rapidly becomes taller, develops larger muscles, and gains weight. His voice begins to change, and underarm hair growth begins. It is at about this same time that the first ejaculation occurs.

Most males have some breast development during puberty. This may be only a button of tissue that can be felt beneath the nipple, which may or may not be tender. Development sometimes is more extensive so the breast protrudes and may be embarrassing. This breast development may be alarming, but in almost all instances, the tissue goes away within a year or two. If it persists, medical advice should be sought.

Most boys are almost at their adult height by seventeen or eighteen, although they may grow a little more after that. Genital development is also essentially complete by this age. Muscle development may progress considerably past eighteen, especially if stimulated by physical work or exercise. Hair on the face, chest, abdomen, and legs may continue to increase over several years.

As you can see, male sexual development is a very complex process, which involves many changes throughout the whole body. It is not uncommon for boys to be alarmed about some of these changes or to fear they are not developing "normally" or "on time." Parents should be sensitive to the possibility of these fears and prepared to alleviate them with the facts. This will require that you take the initiative if you sense your son is worried, since he will probably not initiate the discussion with you. The chances are slim that he will obtain the correct information from other boys. If you feel unable to help your son with these fears, providing him with the opportunity to be alone with your family physician or other counselor is a good idea, as is providing him with reading material that will help ease his mind. Puberty can be upsetting enough without unnecessary worries.

10

Female Sexual Development

As with the preceding chapter on male sexual development, you will probably want to read this material before deciding whether or not to give it to your daughter or son. Since girls begin developing earlier than boys—in most cases between the ages of ten and eleven—they obviously need to know some of this material very early in their lives. If you are not comfortable with the idea of your child reading all of the following material that young, you may want to extract the material you need for your discussion and leave the book itself for a later date. But no matter when you decide to pass this information on to your daughter, it is something she needs to be familiar with sooner or later—maybe sooner than you would like.

The External Genitalia

The female external genitals are called the vulva and are not as conspicuous as those of the male. They include two pairs of lips (labia), the clitoris, and the vaginal opening. The two pairs of lips lie on either side of a midline space. The larger outer lips are the labia majora, making up the two folds of tissue that are the only part of the genitalia readily visible in the prepubertal girl. After puberty, hair covers the outer surface but not the inner surface of the large lips.

In the embryo, genital structures are similar in both sexes. The same structures then develop into those of a boy or girl. The folds that become the labia majora in girls are the same folds that grow together to form the male's scrotum. So, like the scrotum, the outer surface of a girl's labia majora grows hair after puberty and there is a thin layer of muscle in the wall. The inner surface is smooth and hairless, and both surfaces contain oil and sweat glands. Unlike the scrotum, there is a considerable amount of fat tissue within the labia majora, which gives them a fleshy characteristic.

The smaller lips, or labia minora, lie inside the labia majora. The labia majora completely cover the labia minora in the prepubertal child and partially cover those of the mature woman. Within these labia are a core of spongy tissue, a network of fine, elastic fibers, and a large quantity of blood vessels. These vessels, particularly the veins, engorge with blood during sexual excitement, causing the labia to increase considerably in size. There is no hair growth on the labia minora, and they contain no fat cells but do have numerous oil glands.

At the front, the labia minora come together in a fold or hood of skin. Under this fold lies the clitoris. The clitoris is the female counterpart of the penis. Both develop from the same embryonic structure; both are capable of erection and intense sensation. The clitoris is the most highly innervated part of the female genitalia and contains erectile tissue one-half to one inch long, most of which lies deep within the tissues.

Two bodies of erectile tissue, similar to the two cavernous bodies that make up the bulk of the penis, make up the clitoris. The clitoris ends in the glans, which is shaped like a small glans penis without an opening. Most of the clitoris is attached to underlying tissue, with the tip and overlying skin forming a hooded structure. During sexual excitement, the clitoris can become erect because of the trapping of blood. Usually the erect clitoris does not become remarkably longer, but it may become noticeably broader. The glans is covered by a mucous membrane that is continuous with the moist membrane lying between the labia. The clitoris is covered with skin forming what has been called the foreskin of the clitoris, a counterpart of the skin and foreskin covering the penis.

The tissues overlying the erectile tissue of the clitoris are rich in blood vessels and have numerous sensitive nerve fibers with at least three specialized types of nerve endings similar to those found in the penis. These make the clitoris the most sensitive part of female genitalia.

Below the clitoris is the urethral opening, a small opening that is difficult to see. Behind the urethral opening is the vaginal opening called the introitus. The space into which the vagina and urethra open, which is surrounded on the sides by the labia, is called the vestibule. The skin lining the vestibule contains numerous mucous glands concentrated around the clitoris and the opening of the urethra. These mucous glands are similar to those lining the urethra of the penis; in both sexes, they secrete a clear, viscous fluid during sexual excitement. Other larger, lubricating mucous glands are located in the walls of the vestibule and open on the inside of the labia minora. These glands are similar to glands located inside the base of the penis.

The sensitive nerve endings are concentrated not only in the clitoris but also are abundant in the external genital structures, including the vaginal opening. There are not only the usual nerve endings for touch but also two types of specialized sensory endings, one of which is found only in the genital organs and the nipples. There is even a third special nerve structure found deep in the clitoris and the larger lips that is particularly sensitive to pressure changes. Usually the clitoris and inner lips are the most sensitive to touch. With sexual excitement, the nerve stimulation causes secretion of lubricating fluid by the glands and engorgement of the vulva and the vaginal walls, so the genital area becomes redder and thicker.

The Vagina

The vagina is the tubular passageway that leads from the center of the external female genitalia to the internal uterus. The opening of the vagina is not visible unless the labia are parted. In a woman who has never had sexual intercourse, the entrance may be minimally, partially, or (rarely) completely closed by the hymen. This membrane is usually thin and delicate but may occasionally be tough.

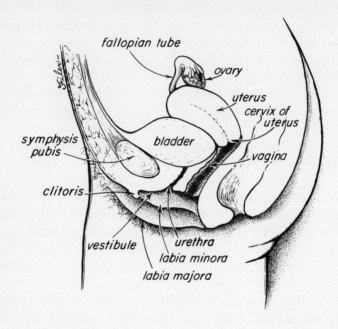

The vagina is the tube into which the penis is inserted during intercourse, into which the sperm is deposited, and which becomes the birth canal.

When not stretched, an adult female's vagina is three to five inches long. Because of secretions, the inside of the vagina is usually soft and moist. The upper end surrounds the cervix or neck of the uterus. A woman who has never been pregnant has a narrow opening in the center of the cervix. After pregnancy, this opening is a horizontal slit rather than a small, round opening.

The walls of the vagina contain interlacing muscle fibers that are arranged both around the tube and along its length. The movement of these muscles cannot be controlled at will but they contract and release in response to autonomous nervous-system stimulation that may be activated during sexual excitement. There is, however, a ring-shaped sphincter of muscle around the vaginal opening that can be tightened and relaxed at will.

Different portions of the vagina vary in sensitivity to touch. Much of it is not particularly sensitive, but the most sensitive area

116

surrounds the opening. The membrane lining the wall of the vagina varies in appearance, secretion, and thickness, depending on the amount and type of hormonal stimulation. In women with regular menstrual cycles, the inside of the vagina is continually changing. Although the lining of the vagina contains cells that secrete mucus, there are actually few glands within the wall of the vagina; most of the mucus for lubricating the vagina comes from the uterine cervix.

The Uterus

The uterus is somewhat pear shaped, although it is flattened front to back. It is three to four inches long in an adult, nonpregnant woman, and has a thick, muscular wall. The muscle layers are a network of flat and round bundles of muscle coursing through strong but stretchable fibers and support tissue. The vagina connects through the opening in the cervix to the cavity inside the uterus. This cavity has a unique lining which prepares each month to accept a fertilized egg. If an egg is not fertilized, the lining is discharged during menstruation.

The Menstrual Cycle

The lining of the uterus is called the endometrium. This lining passes through cyclic changes throughout the menstrual cycle. If an egg has not been fertilized or if that fertilized egg has not implanted into the lining of the uterus and begun to form the fetus and the placenta, the inner lining of the uterus begins to shed about two weeks after ovulation. This bloody menstrual flow is evidence of menstrual cycling and occurs about every four weeks in the nonpregnant, reproductive-aged woman. The discharge through the vagina includes much of the cellular lining of the uterus, secretions from glands that make up some of that lining, and blood from the shedding tissues.

The uterus contains specially designed coiled blood vessels that can contract to cut off the blood flow or dilate to allow blood to escape into the uterine cavity as the lining is being shed. If pregnancy hasn't occurred by two weeks after ovulation, there is a decrease in blood supply to the uterine lining because of constriction of these vessels. The lining begins to disintegrate and starts to slough off once the blood supply to the surface of the endometrium has been cut off. Intermittently after the blood supply is cut off, the vessels briefly open and blood passes into the lining tissue. Pieces of tissue, secretions, and blood pass into the uterine cavity, flow down into the vagina, and out.

This phase of the menstrual cycle is called a period, or menstruation. It lasts from three to six days, usually four to five days. The average loss of blood is about one ounce, but quantity of the menstrual flow varies. Some women have light flow and others have heavy flow, or some women have heavy flow only during part of their periods. The menstrual fluid may contain small clots, most commonly during times of heavy flow. This menstrual flow does not weaken the body unless the person is anemic. It is actually a discard of what is no longer needed. Menstrual pads are worn over the vaginal opening or tampons are inserted into the vagina during a menstrual cycle to absorb the flow.

While the blood loss in an otherwise healthy woman is not great enough to cause weakness, the discomfort or cramps sometimes associated with fluid loss can make a woman feel weak and tired. The causes of this are not well understood, but they are certainly related to the profound hormonal changes occurring during this phase of the cycle. Menstrual cramps are probably related to contractions of the uterus and to the constriction of the vessels cutting off the blood supply to the lining of the uterus. Many women notice no cramps or discomfort at all with their periods, some do occasionally, and some regularly. Those who are bothered the most seem to be those who feel more tired and irritable just before their periods and experience bloating of the legs, abdomen, and breasts.

The actual decreased blood supply and uterine shedding begins when hormone secretion from the ovaries drops markedly. These hormone levels fall about two weeks after ovulation if pregnancy has not begun. The entire menstrual cycle is controlled by hormones secreted by the ovaries. This intricately regulated hormone secretion results in agreement between the phase of the uterine cycle and ovulation, so that when cycles occur normally, the uterine

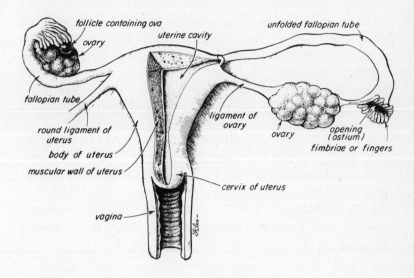

lining is ready to receive and nourish a fertilized egg at the same time a mature egg is released by the ovary.

By the time the menstrual flow has stopped, cells have begun to grow over the lining of the uterus as the beginning of a new cycle. This regrowth phase is called the preovulatory phase. It lasts about ten days in women who cycle regularly, but it may be shorter or much longer. During this time, the lining thickens and the glands regrow and accumulate secretion. This phase corresponds with the follicular phase of the ovary when a follicle and its enclosed egg are maturing. It ends when ovulation occurs. The length of time between menstruation and ovulation determines the length of the whole menstrual cycle. After ovulation, it is generally two weeks until a woman's next period. By the end of the preovulatory phase, there is more secretion by the glands and more fluid accumulated within the uterine lining, so it is prepared to receive a fertilized egg.

Following ovulation, the secretion from the glands is greater, thicker, and more mucous. Thus, the next phase is called the secretory or premenstrual phase. The lining of the uterus at this time provides the perfect environment for the fertilized egg. This condition is maintained by hormones from the ovaries and persists for about two weeks if pregnancy has not occurred. If the hormones of pregnancy haven't begun to be produced in those two weeks, there is a dramatic hormonal drop, resulting in a decreased blood supply to the lining. This begins the sequence leading to the next menstrual period, and the cycle is complete. This cycling of the lining of the uterus usually recurs again and again throughout a woman's reproductive years, unless she becomes pregnant.

Occasionally cycles stop or become irregular especially in teenage girls during the first few years after the first period. Although a period suggests that ovulation has occurred, it is not necessarily so. If periods become very infrequent, too frequent, or last too long, a woman should consult her doctor. Of course periods stop naturally at menopause, sometimes abruptly and sometimes after becoming irregular.

The Fallopian Tubes

Arising from each side of the uterus and extending to the ovary on each side are the oviducts or fallopian tubes. These tubes lie within the ligaments that attach the ovary to the uterus. The fallopian tubes are muscular tubes about five inches long and less than one-half inch thick. At one end, the lining of the tube connects with the lining of the uterus. The other end contains many fingerlike projections that extend over the ovary.

The function of the oviduct is to carry the egg to the uterus, and its lining is constructed in folds running lengthwise to help move the egg along. The cells that make up the lining are of two specially designed types. One type bears little hairlike cilia that beat in waves toward the uterus, helping to carry the egg in the right direction. Other cells in the lining of the oviduct secrete a substance that coats the egg and eases its movement. There is a muscle layer in the oviduct made up of muscle fibers arranged in a spiral configuration and others arranged along the length of the oviduct. These muscle fibers are thickest near the uterus.

At the time of ovulation, the oviduct and the ovary actively move.

Between the strands of muscle at the opening of the oviduct is an array of blood vessels forming a ring. When ovulation occurs, these vessels become filled with blood and the enlarged end of the oviduct forms a funnel that fits over the ovary. Rhythmic contractions of the oviduct occur in the direction of the uterus, while the waves of cilia beat in the same direction to carry the egg.

If the ovulated egg is fertilized, the actual union of the egg and sperm usually occurs while the egg is passing along the oviduct. The egg immediately begins to divide. It moves into the uterine cavity and implants itself into the prepared uterine lining, which is at its thickest at this time. The outer cells of the dividing egg develop into the placenta, which takes over hormone production so there isn't a drop of hormone levels two weeks after ovulation, as there would be normally. These hormones maintain the lining of the uterus and prevent menstruation. For the next nine months, the placenta produces massive quantities of hormones that support the pregnancy. Throughout the pregnancy, the placenta obtains nutrients and oxygen for the baby from the mother's blood supply and transfers fetal wastes back to the mother's blood for elimination.

The Ovaries

The ovaries are paired and lie on either side of the uterus at the end of the fallopian tubes in the lower part of the abdomen. Each ovary is covered by a clear sheet of tissue and is attached by a stem. The surface that is not attached bulges from the back wall of the abdomen into the abdominal cavity, where it is connected to the uterus by a ligament. The ovaries grow gradually throughout childhood, so by age five they are five or six times as heavy as at birth. For several years before puberty they grow more slowly and then grow rapidly to adult size during puberty.

Adult ovaries are somewhat flattened, bean-shaped oval structures one to two inches long, one-half to one and a quarter inches wide, and up to one-half inch thick. They contain many various-sized follicles in which eggs develop. The size of an ovary varies from one month to the next because the most mature follicles may become as big as one-half inch in diameter. When a follicle fully matures, it ruptures onto the surface of the ovary, releasing the egg into the oviduct. After ovulation, the follicle becomes a temporary hormone-producing gland that secretes large amounts of hormone to prepare the uterine lining for pregnancy. This secretion lasts about two weeks.

When a girl is born, each ovary already contains 300,000 to 400,000 or more eggs. No new eggs are formed after birth, in contrast to sperm, which are produced by the millions throughout life. The number of eggs in the ovary decreases progressively throughout life, and only 300 to 400 will mature. Follicles continue to grow and mature until menopause. Throughout childhood, the follicles develop only partially, but once sexual maturity is attained, an egg matures and is ovulated each month unless a woman is pregnant, ill, or taking hormones—such as birth control pills.

Ovulation occurs about halfway between menstrual periods. The mature egg is in a mature follicle, which is a fluid-filled cyst. The cyst ruptures and the fluid flows out, carrying the egg with it. The egg normally is directed into the fallopian tube by the fingerlike structures extending over the ovary on the end of the tube. It is carried down the tube for about three days. If it is not fertilized by the time it reaches the uterus, the egg disintegrates. Ovulation is usually painless, and a woman is normally not aware of it. Occasionally there may be acute pain or discomfort of short duration. Ovulation is caused by a sudden spike in hormone levels and may be accompanied by midcycle spotting of blood from the vagina.

Menopause occurs because the ovaries contain no more follicles to produce hormones and no more maturing eggs. This may happen suddenly or may take the form of less-frequent periods over time before complete cessation. Because of hormone imbalance at this time, growth of the uterine lining may be abnormal and some women's periods may become excessively heavy, requiring medical attention.

Puberty

Over the last century, puberty has begun progressively earlier in both sexes. This is probably the result of better socioeconomic conditions, particularly better nutrition. Puberty in most girls begins with breast development, followed within months by growth of the first pubic hairs. Occasionally, pubic hair may be the first sign of puberty. In girls, puberty may begin as early as age eight or as late as thirteen or fourteen, but in most the onset is between the tenth and eleventh birthdays. Breast development starts with an elevation of the nipple and surrounding breast tissue and an increase in the diameter of the areolae, the pigmented circles of skin around the nipples. The growth of breasts may begin on one side before the other, and differences in breast size may persist for some time past puberty.

The growth of pigmented pubic hairs usually occurs first along the labia majora. Hair then spreads up above the genitals, sometimes expenting laterally to the hips or thighs but only occasionally up to the abdomen.

Pubertal genital development begins at the same time or shortly after breast and pubic hair growth begins. The labia, particularly the labia minora, develop considerably and become more prominent. They may become more deeply pigmented and grow so they show between the labia majora. The lining of the vagina changes, becoming thicker and moister. There is more mucus secretion, and there may be a clear or whitish discharge.

Girls develop adult-type body odor at or before the growth of pubic hair; underarm hair begins to grow a year or two later. Acne may become a problem during middle or late puberty, especially just before or during periods.

Breasts and pubic hair develop over several years, more rapidly for some than for others. The most common time interval from the onset of puberty to full adult development is three to three and a half years. However, some females may become fully developed within about two years, or normal development may be prolonged over a six- to eight-year period.

The characteristic female changes in the physique and body contours begin during early puberty. A girl's pubertal growth spurt begins at about the same time as her first signs of puberty, while boys don't begin their rapid growth until midpuberty. Maximum weight gain and height increase has already occurred in most girls by the time boys begin to grow. This difference in size and development obviously adds to the social awkwardness between the sexes at this time.

Maximum growth in height occurs at about the twelfth birthday in a typical girl. Peak growth rates are, on an average, three and a half inches a year. The time of greatest weight gain is in the first half of the thirteenth year, with the beginning of the mature female distribution around the hips, thighs, and buttocks.

Menstrual periods usually begin near midpuberty. The average age for the first period, called the menarche, is twelve and a half to thirteen years, although it may be as early as ten or as late as sixteen. The first period occurs about two years after a girl's breast development begins, but it may occasionally occur sooner or not until several years later. This first period does not necessarily mean that ovulation has occurred. It does mean that the lining of the uterus had been stimulated to grow by the presence of female hormones.

The average girl grows two or more inches after her periods begin, although variation is considerable, with some growing up to five inches. Others, especially those who do not begin to menstruate until they are older, may grow less than an inch.

Ovulation, and thus the potential for fertility, may have occurred two weeks before the first period, and regular ovulation and monthly cycles may occur from the very first period. In many females, however, regular ovulatory cycling may not start for several years. Since irregular periods are as common as regular ones, girls should not be concerned if they are irregular for the first several years. Most regularly cycling teenagers have a period every three to five weeks. Periods may be light or heavy, may be painless or accompanied by cramps, and may last two to seven days, with four to five days being most common.

Throughout puberty between periods, a girl may have a whitish or clear vaginal secretion. This is evidence of normal pubertal development. The nature and amount of this secretion varies at different times between periods, and it may be clearer and greater in amount at midcycle.

With the onset of puberty, females do not experience as dramatic an increase of sexual interest or drive as males, although both sexes are capable of orgasm before puberty. The dramatic upsurge of drive in males accompanies their development of the capacity for ejaculation. A female's interest is more diffuse and is usually directed toward males in general, while a male's interest tends to have a clearly overt sexual awareness.

Each person is responsible for her own health and should make it a habit to take care of herself physically. This begins with good hygiene and regular adequate sleeping hours. Regular medical checkups are important, although much more important after age forty and even more so after age fifty. However, because cancer is a possibility in anyone it is wise and lifesaving to be sure it is found early. Each woman should ask her doctor for recommendations about breast and pelvic examinations and for signs that should alert one to get a check-up.

Mature girls and women should learn how to examine their own breasts for any unusual irregularities or lumps that could indicate an abnormality including early signs of breast cancer. Early discovery of such conditions can be made by the woman herself; with prompt treatment, there is an excellent chance of a cure. Self-examination should be done regularly on a monthly basis about a week after the menstrual period. Many women are reluctant to examine their own breasts because they don't know what to feel for. The American Cancer Society has a free booklet that covers the procedure for breasts self-examination. It basically indicates the following: If you do find a lump or notice a discharge from the nipple, it's important to see your doctor as soon as possible. Most breast lumps are not cancerous, but only your doctor is qualified to make this diagnosis.

To examine your own breasts, follow these three steps.

1. In the shower: Keeping fingers flat, move them gently over every part of each breast. Use the right hand to examine your left breast, the left hand for the right breast. Check for lumps or thickening. A ridge of firm tissue in the lower curve of each breast is normal.

2. Before a mirror: Put your arms at your sides. Next raise your arms overhead. Look for changes in the contour of each breast,

125

a swelling, dimpling of the skin, or changes in the nipple. Then rest your palms on your hips and press them down firmly as you flex or tighten your chest muscles. Look again for the same signs as above. Realize that normally the right and left breast when viewed this way will not exactly match.

3. Lying down: To examine your right breast, put a pillow or folded towel under your right shoulder. Place your right hand behind your head to distribute breast tissue more evenly on your chest. With your left hand, fingers flat, press the breast gently in small circular motions along the base of the breast. Then move up an inch, repeat and continue to use circular movements to examine every part of your breast, including the nipple. To do an adequate job you need to use the circle technique for five or more circles. Repeat the same procedure slowly and carefully on your entire left breast. To complete the exam, squeeze each nipple gently between thumb and index finger. If there is any discharge or fluid expressed from the breast, you should report it to your doctor immediately. If you find any lump, thickening, swelling, puckering, dimpling, or any redness, tenderness, pain, or irritation, you should notify your doctor immediately. Although these things are usually false alarms, if they are a sign of trouble, the problem can be cured if found soon enough!

11

Birth Control, Infertility, and Disease

Understanding contraception and methods of birth control is part of sex education. If you are the parent of a teenager, it is part of your responsibility to discuss the whole concept of responsible parenthood. Unless you believe that sex is meant only for reproduction, it makes sense that most of the time pregnancy should be avoided. So your teenager should learn about birth control as part of preparation for adulthood. As we have already discussed, this doesn't carry a double message if your position on sex outside of marriage is clear. Teaching teenagers about birth control doesn't have to imply to them that even though you tell them not to have sex, you really expect they are going to anyway.

Any two people engaging in sexual activity should be willing to accept the responsibility of parenthood. This does not imply that contraceptive measures should be avoided. On the contrary, a sense of responsibility most of the time implies just the opposite. Because of the demands of parenthood and the stress and wear on the mother's body, most couples choose to limit the number of children they have so they can plan to provide for each of them adequately. Couples just starting their marriage often want to delay parenthood while they adjust to their new life-style. Later, couples may want to space the births of their children. Many concerns, including finances, result in a couple's desire to limit the total number of children they have. And, of course, there is an age beyond which a couple would not choose to have more children.

Contraceptive methods need to be considered because pregnancy will result within a year for 80 percent of sexually active couples who do not use contraception. There are various methods available, although none is ideal. Many methods can be chosen and obtained by the couple themselves, some require a doctor's fitting or prescription. A combination of two or more methods can be used to be virtually certain that pregnancy will not result. However, the biggest factor in the reliability of any method is its consistent and careful utilization every time by the couple.

Birth Control

Condom

The oldest method of birth control is the condom, a sheath worn over the penis during intercourse. This originated as early as 1700 but it became generally available about a hundred years ago when the process of vulcanizing rubber made mass production possible. Worldwide, the condom is the most commonly used effective form of contraception. It's cheap and can be purchased without a prescription. It also has the added feature of protecting against sexually transmitted diseases. With proper use it can be effective against conception 97 percent of the time. This figure, however, does not mean that pregnancy results three times out of one hundred instances of intercourse. It is based on pregnancies per years of usage.

Condoms are rolled when purchased. The rolled condom is placed over the end of the penis and unrolled down over the penis. Some condoms come with a reservoir for semen at the tip. If there is not a reservoir, about a half an inch should be left at the tip to prevent semen from being forced between the shaft of the penis and the sheath and possibly leaking out at the base. After ejaculation, the penis should be removed before the erection fades, while holding the condom by the base to prevent it from slipping off.

Contraceptive Creams, Jellies, or Foams

Vaginal spermicides contain chemicals that stop the sperm from fertilizing the egg by interfering with their ability to move or live. While they can be used alone, they are not as reliable as other methods because adequate amounts may not be in the right place at the right time. They are of great value in conjunction with other forms of birth control, particularly the diaphragm and the condom, providing extra protection by killing sperm in the vagina. They also serve as a lubricant. They can be purchased without a prescription and must be used immediately before intercourse, carefully following the directions that come with them.

The Diaphragm

The diaphragm is a rubber cap placed over the cervix before intercourse, in combination with spermicidal cream or jelly. Used properly, the diaphragm is 97 percent effective. A doctor fits each individual woman with the correct size diaphragm and provides instructions for its use, which are fairly simple.

Since it may be inserted up to three hours before sex, the diaphragm doesn't need to interfere with lovemaking. After intercourse, it must be left in for eight hours to be sure all the sperm are destroyed, and certain precautions must be taken to assure that the diaphragm is properly cared for when not in use.

The Cervical Cap

The Food and Drug Administration has recently approved the cervical cap, which is widely used in Europe, for distribution in the United States. The cap is only about half the size of the diaphragm and is easier to use. When used in conjunction with spermicides, it is as effective as the diaphragm. Like the diaphragm, the cervical cap must be fitted by a doctor, but it may be left in for forty-eight hours. Whether it will become a reasonable alternative is yet to be proven. In a small percentage of women it causes changes in the cells of the cervix. These changes show up on a Pap smear, which is

the examination of cells from the uterine cervix under the micro-
scope and should be part of an annual examination of every adult
woman. Changes in the cells may mean early cancerous changes but
not necessarily so. Women using the cervical cap should have
regular Pap smears.

The Pill

Birth control pills have been in use since the 1950s. They work on
the principle that the hormones estrogen and progesterone stop the
maturation and ovulation of the egg during each cycle. When taken
as prescribed, the pill is almost 100 percent effective in preventing
pregnancy. However, its use is accompanied by some risk to the
woman's health. Birth control pills are safest for use by young
healthy women and should be avoided by women who have any
breast, uterine, heart, or blood vessel problems. Women who use
the pill are more prone to blood-clot disorders and smoking adds to
this risk.

Pills have to be prescribed. When a woman consults a doctor and
receives a prescription she should find out what symptoms may
signal problems. With proper medical supervision, the birth control
pill can be a most effective type of contraception for a limited
number of years. It is usually safer for older women to use some
other method.

Sterilization

Sterilization is an option for couples who are absolutely sure they
want no more children. If either partner has doubts of any kind, it's
best not to have it done, since operations to reverse sterilization
rarely work.

A woman is sterilized by tubal ligation. Tubal ligation involves the
cutting and tying off of both fallopian tubes. It can be done in the
hospital following the birth of a child, when the tubes are high in
the abdomen and easier to reach. It can also be done in the doctor's
office under local anesthetic using a laparoscope, an instrument that
requires only a small incision, making it a fairly simple and painless

operation. Sometimes it can be done through the vagina so an incision through the skin isn't necessary. Tubal ligation does not change the woman's monthly cycle or interfere with hormone production—it just makes it impossible for sperm and egg to meet.

A man is sterilized by vasectomy, an operation performed in the doctor's office or outpatient clinic under local anesthetic. In a vasectomy a small opening is made in the scrotal skin on each side and the cord or vas deferens is located. A section of each cord is removed. This prevents the sperm from leaving the scrotum. They continue to be formed but are gradually reabsorbed by the body. All in all, a vasectomy is considerably easier and safer than a tubal ligation. The failure rate is only about two per one thousand men, when a new channel develops; the larger the section of the vas deferens removed, the less the chance is of this happening.

Sterilization is not immediately complete with a vasectomy because sperm may be present in the ducts beyond the place where the piece is removed. It may take six to eight weeks, depending on the frequency of intercourse, and a semen sample must be checked for sperm before assuming infertility. Once the semen is sperm-free, there is virtually no chance of conception.

Some men fear that a vasectomy will affect their sex drive, but there is no physical basis for this fear. Ejaculation and the physical sensations of sex are unchanged. The only change is that sperm are not present in the semen.

The Intrauterine Device (IUD)

The IUD is a device inserted into the woman's uterus by her doctor. When it became available in the mid-sixties, it was accepted without much concern about how it avoided pregnancy. The IUD does not prevent conception, the union of the egg and sperm, but stops a fertilized egg from implanting itself in the uterus's lining. If birth control prevents the union, one doesn't have to be concerned about when the newly formed organism becomes a person—when the body is indwelt by a soul. Christians have moral reservations about any form of birth control that affects a fertilized egg—unlike

131

those that prevent egg and sperm from meeting—and the IUD is problematic from that standpoint.

There are also severe medical problems with IUDs that should be considered. Complications include infections, perforation of the uterine wall, ectopic pregnancy, excessive bleeding, and abortion. All things considered, the IUD is not a recommended form of contraception.

Natural Family Planning

So-called natural family planning revolves around the fact that the egg lives for only twenty-four hours and sperm for forty-eight to seventy-two hours. This means there are only a limited number of days a month when a woman can conceive, and if intercourse is avoided during that time, conception will not take place. The problem is that it is difficult to determine when ovulation will occur. After ovulation the body temperature rises slightly, so by taking a basal temperature daily before getting out of bed, the day of ovulation may be detected. Of course, that doesn't help much if the couple had intercourse the night before. By counting days and taking basal temperatures, a couple at best will need to avoid intercourse for ten days each cycle, about a third of the time. It is obvious why the failure rate is high for this method.

Abortion

Abortion is a fact of life in today's world, but the truth is, abortion is not contraception. Few Christians support it or would want someone they love to experience it. Unexpected pregnancies happen to Christians as well as non-Christians, so parents opposed to abortion must be willing to provide whatever help or support their children need if, despite everything, one of them faces a surprise pregnancy. Dealing with this event is traumatic for everyone concerned. How you handle it may prove to be the ultimate test of both your faith and your love for your children. In the long run, most feel they did the better thing not to terminate the pregnancy but to have the child and give it for adoption to some couple who desperately want a child.

Infertility

Infertility is the inability of a couple to have children; by definition it is the lack of conception after a full year of intercourse without the use of birth control. Infertility can be a terrible blow to a couple that want to have children. However, up to half of all couples who have been unsuccessful within one year can have children with proper medical guidance. No couple should abandon the hope of having children before exploring all the medical possibilities.

Many factors can be responsible for a couple's infertility. A woman may have a hormone imbalance, an infection or inflammation, or blocked fallopian tubes. A man can have an infection or a hormone imbalance, be taking medicines that interfere, or have an anatomic problem, such as varicocele (abnormally dilated blood vessels) in the scrotum.

The initial medical evaluation includes checking out simple things. Is the woman having regular periods, and is she ovulating? Is the man ejaculating at the right time and in the right place? What is the frequency of intercourse? It can be too often or too seldom for optimal conditions for conception. How long has the couple been having regular intercourse without contraception? What positions are used? Is lubricating jelly used and, if so, what kind? Does the wife douche right after intercourse?

More complicated testing involves checking the husband's hormone levels and semen. The number, shape, and activity of sperm are evaluated. The woman can have hormonal testing, chemical tests to see how her system affects sperm mobility, and evaluation to be sure the fallopian tubes are open.

If the couple is not among the one-third to one-half that can be helped, there are other possible alternatives. While most people have no moral reservations about any of the methods described above, some alternatives can be problematic and require the couple's thoughtful and prayerful consideration. Some may not even be up for consideration. Neither partner should be emotionally pressured into a decision that offends his or her moral standards. If there is ever a time for thorough, considerate communication between husband and wife, it is with this type of decision.

Artificial Insemination

Artificial insemination involves the mechanical placement of a sperm sample at the ideal time for conception. Concentrated sperm samples can be used. Each year, 10,000 to 20,000 babies are born in the United States through artificial insemination. Most people have no problems with this technique if the husband's sperm is used.

Artificial insemination takes place in the physician's office at the time of the woman's ovulation. The doctor inserts part of the husband sperm sample with a syringe, then places a plastic pessary containing the rest of the sample in the vagina. This must stay in place for six to eight hours. The process is painless but may have to be repeated two or three times before conception.

Artificial insemination with donor sperm not from the husband causes difficulties for many people, including religious leaders, who are divided on the question. Christian couples considering this should discuss all the issues with each other and with other Christians whose viewpoints they respect.

In Vitro Fertilization

In vitro fertilization involves the fertilization of the woman's egg outside her body and the subsequent placement of the conceptus back into her womb. This technique makes it possible for a woman with damaged or blocked fallopian tubes to conceive and carry her own baby to term. It also may be used in women who have a hormone imbalance. Hormones can be given for weeks or months according to a careful schedule in order to mature eggs in a woman who does not ovulate spontaneously. Eggs can be harvested from the ovaries, fertilized, and placed in the uterus. The techniques are difficult and several tries may be necessary before pregnancy is achieved. On the other hand, several eggs may be fertilized and grow so twins, triplets, or more may result.

Surrogate Mothering

In surrogate mothering, the husband's or a donor's sperm are used to impregnate a volunteer mother, who then gives the child up for adoption by the father and his infertile wife. While there are very few technical difficulties with this technique, the legal and moral consequences are profound and not many Christians support surrogate mothering as a viable option for parenthood.

Adoption

Although adoption is a totally acceptable means of becoming a parent, social changes, mainly abortion, have made it less available as an option for infertile couples. In addition to availability of abortion, modern contraceptives and the current trend for single mothers to keep their children have greatly reduced the available number of adoptable infants. Older children, those with handicaps, and orphans from overseas are more readily available, if the couple is prepared for the extra care and effort these children often require. The social and psychological implications of adopting a child of a different race, culture, and background must be realistically considered.

A Childless Life?

Some couples will eventually have to accept the fact that they will never have children of their own. Once the pain and disappointment subside, many will find useful outlets for their love of children, such as involving themselves in volunteer work or close relationships with children of their relatives and friends. These days, there are millions of children who desperately need the love and attention of adults, and many agencies that would be delighted to find mature, willing helpers. While working with others' children may never totally satisfy the childless couple, the rewards to be gained are many and precious.

Sexually Transmitted Diseases

Sexually transmitted diseases have plagued mankind for hundreds of years, with mentions of syphilis appearing in European literature shortly after Columbus's voyage to the New World. Early skeletal remains of Columbian natives showed evidence of syphilis, so for many years it was considered a New World disease brought back to Europe by explorers. However, there is evidence that many cases of Old World leprosy, going back to long before 1500, may actually have been syphilis, since leprosy was then considered highly contagious (which it isn't) and was associated with sexual contact. Sexually transmitted diseases have been around for a long time. The major long-known diseases killed vast numbers of people before the appearance of modern antibiotics. Common sexually transmitted diseases include syphilis, gonorrhea, genital herpes, lymphogranuloma venereum (chlamydia), trichomonas, granuloma inguinale, condyloma acuminatum, and molluscum contagiosum.

Pelvic inflammatory disease (PID) refers to infection of the fallopian tubes and uterus of women. It may be caused by several factors, commonly by sexually transmitted disease. There are over a million cases in the United States each year. It is more common in young women who have never had children and who have multiple sexual partners. Two common causes of PID are gonorrhea and chlamydia although only some of those with genital infection develop PID. It may be suspected if abdominal pain develops in a sexually active female. However, there may be no symptoms, especially with chlamydia infections. The infection may result in scarring and blockage of the fallopian tubes resulting in infertility. More than 10 percent of women become infertile after one episode and 50 percent or more after three or more episodes. Sexually transmitted diseases in males may also result in infertility by causing a blockage of the sperm ducts.

Syphilis is a bacterial infection. It has diverse symptoms and long periods of no symptoms. Its first symptom appears two to four weeks after sexual contact with an infected person and consists of a painless lump on the genitalia, around the anus, or in the mouth. This lump breaks down into an ulcer. Syphilis can be detected in its earliest stage through microscopic examination; several weeks later it can be diagnosed by blood tests. In the secondary state, it causes raised nodules in the genital area. Syphilis is treated with massive doses of penicillin and is curable in its early stages. The later stages result in severe nerve damage. Untreated women generally pass the disease on to their unborn children.

Gonorrhea, the most common venereal disease, also is caused by bacteria. The earliest symptom noticed is a painful burning sensation while urinating. Untreated, gonorrhea will spread, infecting the male's urethra, prostate, and seminal vesicles and possibly causing sterility. In women symptoms may not occur until a large, painful abscess has formed near the vagina or it has spread to the fallopian tubes. Infection of the tubes can cause them to scar and blockage results in infertility. The bacteria can be identified in samples of urethral or vaginal discharge and treated with antibiotics.

Genital herpes infection is a common genital disease, particularly in sexually active adolescents. Most genital infections are caused by a herpes virus different from the one that causes herpes infections of the mouth (commonly called cold sores or fever blisters). Often infection is obvious because a painful sore develops on the genitals. It becomes a blister and then forms a crust. Sometimes, however, particularly when the infection involves the internal genitals, such as the cervix of the uterus, it is difficult to diagnose because the typical sore does not develop. Once a person is infected with the virus, sores may come and go, and recurrence is common. Although the sores clear up spontaneously in about fourteen days, the virus remains inactive and then may become active again and again. There is no known cure for herpes. When sores are present, the herpes is very infectious. The rate of infection during asymptomatic periods is less but unknown.

Lymphogranuloma venereum is a sexually transmitted disease caused by bacteria known as chlamydia. It has become less prevalent in the United States, probably because of improved hygiene, although it remains common in developing countries. It is more common in males. It begins as a simple pimple or a small ulcer on the penis or vagina. Later, lymph nodes in the area become enlarged. Eventually strictures and sores are formed in the genital and rectal areas. Treatment is by antibiotics.

Trichomonas is a common sexually transmitted disease in teenagers and adults. It is caused by a protozoan and can take days or weeks to develop. Because it may remain dormant for months, an individual can infect sexual partners without even knowing he or she is infected. It may cause pain and itching and a discharge.

Granuloma inguinale is caused by a bacterium that is transmitted by sexual intercourse. This disease develops insidiously and is relatively painless. It involves the development of ulcers and can result in scar tissue formation on the genitalia. It is treated with antibiotics.

Chancroid is rare but very painful from the time the sore develops. It first appears two to fourteen days after exposure through intercourse, in the form of a small red pimple on the genitals. It soon becomes filled with pus and then decays into an ulceration. Other pimples may then appear. Chancroid is diagnosed through a laboratory culture and then treated with antibiotics. The incidence has become more common in the last few years.

Condyloma acuminatum are known as venereal warts. There may be only a single wart or a cluster of warts growing together. They are caused by a virus different from those responsible for common warts. This sexually transmitted disease has become much more common in the United States today. It may take two to six months to develop. Treatment involves removing the warts by surgery or electrocauterization. The warts may reappear after the first treatment so therapy may need to be repeated.

Molluscum contagiosum is a disease caused by a virus that may be sexually transmitted but usually is spread in a more general way. It occurs in children. It forms a characteristic papule which can resolve on its own but may require removal. It does not have aftereffects.

AIDS

Today's most threatening sexually transmitted disease (although it can also be transmitted in other ways) is *acquired immune deficiency syndrome* (AIDS), a disease caused by a virus (the human immunodeficiency virus—HIV) that eventually destroys the body's ability to fight even the most minor infection. Bacteria, yeasts, or other infectious agents which are everywhere and don't affect the normal person, can kill the person whose natural defense mechanisms are destroyed. The natural course of the disease is progressive weakness with chronic infections that do not develop in a healthy person. Some of these infectious agents are resistant to antibiotics, are persistent, and eventually cause death.

Although it was first recognized in Africa as a disease among heterosexuals, AIDS was first seen in America as a threat to male homosexuals. AIDS is transmitted by the exchange of body fluids, primarily semen or blood. The most dangerous homosexual act is anal-rectal intercourse, and the partner most at risk is the passive one. The anus and rectum are not designed to withstand dilation and friction the way the vagina is, and the movement of the sex act can produce tears and bruises in the wall of the lower digestive tract. Even if there is no damage, semen and other fluids are fairly readily absorbed through the digestive wall, which, unlike the vaginal wall, is permeable. The rectum may contain molecules that chemically attach to the virus. Thus, if semen contaminated with the HIV virus gets inside the rectum, it may spread throughout the body, where it can begin its destructive process.

Although the HIV virus may be found in any body fluid, it is primarily carried from person to person in semen or blood. This is why homosexual males and IV drug users who share needles are at the greatest risk. Homosexual males are still more at risk than other

139

groups because of contact with semen, and the more partners such a person has, the more likely he is to be infected. Homosexual females are at low risk, but individuals of both sexes who have multiple sexual partners have a clearly increased risk. Women having sexual relations with multiple or casual acquaintances are most at risk because it is not apparent who the infected males are. Newborn children of infected mothers are likely to have acquired the disease before birth. Studies have shown that AIDS is not transmitted by casual contact. Families of AIDS victims do not catch it from them. Kissing, hugging, and using public facilities do not seem to transmit the disease.

One of the main dangers of AIDS is its long latency period before symptoms begin to appear—perhaps as long as ten to fifteen years. Since AIDS is a danger to heterosexuals as well as homosexuals with multiple partners, the only truly safe course is chastity—abstention before marriage and faithfulness after.

It is important for informed Christians to know about diseases that may be transmitted primarily by physically intimate sexual contact, especially AIDS. It is just as important that children and teenagers realize that if they are not sexually intimate before marriage and have sex only with their spouses after marriage, they do not have to worry about getting AIDS or any other sexually transmitted diseases. Using condoms or anything else is not a guarantee that a person won't catch AIDS or other diseases from an infected partner. You can't tell who is infected and the more sexual partners a person has the more likely he is to contact someone who is infected. Many adults today are worried that their early sexual activities may have exposed them to AIDS. They worry because they know AIDS may take years to develop. On the other hand, many adults who did not have sex before marriage and who have remained faithful since marriage are very thankful that they did not expose themselves. In this way, having lived a life of chastity added a worry-free dimension to their lives.

12

Pregnancy and Childbirth

There is no experience in life that quite matches the thrill of parenthood. It is elating to think that intercourse, the completely enjoyable expression of love, caring, and commitment can result in a child, a gift and a trust from God.

Once each month a woman releases a mature egg from one of her ovaries. This happens about halfway through the menstrual cycle. During the first half the body produces the hormones that cause the egg to mature and ovulation to happen. Right after the egg is released the ovary begins to make hormones that prepare the uterus to receive the fertilized egg. Sperm, of course, are produced regularly by the millions.

Pregnancy occurs when an egg and sperm meet, usually high in the fallopian tube. Although an unfertilized egg will live for only twenty-four hours or so, sperm live for at least two to three days, making conception possible only when intercourse occurs during those particular days each month. Millions of sperm may reach the egg, but only one actually enters it, carrying the father's genetic material, part of which determines the sex of the child. Once the sperm enters the egg, its tail drops off and its head moves toward the center of the egg, where its genetic material joins with that from the mother and the resulting conceptus begins to divide and form into a cluster of bubblelike cells.

This cell division continues as the fertilized egg makes its way down the fallopian tube. On the fourth day, it enters the uterus, which has been prepared to receive it. The egg has already grown to twice the size of an unfertilized egg. It adheres to and begins to implant itself in the uterine lining, which will nourish it until the placenta takes over in the fourth week.

Changes in the Pregnant Woman's Body

Most women can take missing a period as a possible indication of pregnancy. In addition, a woman may notice that her breasts feel full and have become tender, and she may experience nausea and vomiting especially in the morning. As the early pregnancy continues, the enlarging uterus will begin to press on her bladder, causing frequent urination. The woman may also feel drowsy and tired, find she can't tolerate the taste or smell of foods she previously enjoyed, and experience pulling pains in the side of her abdomen as the growing uterus stretches the ligaments that support it. Most of these symptoms will disappear during the second three months as the fetus grows and moves out of the pelvic area, but they may return in the last three months of the pregnancy.

Other signs of pregnancy will be noticed by the woman's doctor. The areola—the area around the nipple—will darken and oil (sebaceous) glands in the area will be more prominent. The tissues of the vulva, vagina, and cervix will darken, and the cervix and uterus will soften.

Normally the uterus is a thick-walled, pear-shaped organ about 3 inches long, weighing about an ounce. During pregnancy, it increases in size until it is about 12 inches long, weighs 2.6 pounds, and holds 4.2 to 5.3 quarts. This increase in size is partly due to an increase in muscle fibers, nerves, lymphatic vessels, and blood vessels in the uterine wall.

By the fourteenth week of pregnancy, the uterus has softened and become flattened and spherical in shape. As the pregnancy continues, the uterus rises up out of the pelvis and fills the abdominal cavity, moving other organs out of its way. As delivery approaches, the uterus becomes top-heavy and falls forward; then, several weeks before delivery, the fetal head descends into the pelvis and the uterus sinks downward.

At term, the placenta connecting the mother to the baby has grown to become a disk 6 to 7 inches in diameter. It is 1 to 1.5 inches thick at its thickest point, and weighs 1 to 2 pounds. It is attached to the wall of the uterus and connects with the baby by the umbilical cord.

A pregnant woman's entire body is affected in one way or another by a pregnancy. After about thirty weeks of pregnancy up until delivery, the load on the mother's heart is heaviest, and it will be doing 25 to 30 percent more work than normal, even though it has been pushed upward to the left and slightly forward by the growing fetus. Blood flow to and from the lower extremities slows, contributing to the swelling of the legs and varicose veins common during later pregnancy. The amount of air moved in and out of the lungs per minute increases during pregnancy until, immediately before delivery, a woman is breathing twice as fast as usual.

As pregnancy progresses, the stomach and intestines lose some of their elasticity, causing some women to complain of indigestion, heartburn, constipation, or hemorrhoids. Pregnancy usually causes the oil and sweat glands in the skin to produce more, hair to become thinner and more brittle, and fingernails to break more easily. Stretch marks appear on the breasts and abdomen. Although they will fade after delivery, they never completely go away.

Early pregnancy is often accompanied by a slight weight loss due to lack of appetite and nausea, but most women gain twenty pounds or more between their third and ninth months. A gain of one pound per week during pregnancy is considered ideal, although some doctors allow more or recommend less, based on the woman's size. At birth, the woman will lose about fifteen pounds; five more will go as her uterus shrinks, but any weight gain in excess of twenty pounds will be lost only through dieting.

This catalog of changes is not meant to be discouraging—many women breeze through pregnancy without being bothered by most of these changes. A woman in reasonably good health who takes care of herself actually may find herself feeling better than ever. Certain life changes may be necessary during pregnancy however. In addition to watching her weight and nutrition, a pregnant woman should not smoke, drink, or use any medication that is not approved by her obstetrician, since all these factors can affect the developing fetus.

The physical expression of love, including intercourse, is just as important or more so during pregnancy. Intercourse is possible throughout most of pregnancy, but you should check with your doctor about when or whether you should avoid it as the end of pregnancy approaches. Different positions may be used for comfort and to avoid pressure on the uterus. Both the husband and wife should continue to celebrate their marriage sexually.

Fetal Development

There are normally 266 to 270 days between ovulation and birth, although there may be as few as 250 or as many as 285. Since it's difficult to determine exactly when ovulation occurred, doctors add 7 days to the first day of the last menstrual period and count forward nine months (or back three months) to set a woman's due date (280 days from the start of the last period). This date is not exact, and delivery slightly before or after 280 days should not be a cause for concern, since only 5 percent of all babies are born on their due dates. So to be realistic, a woman should expect to deliver anytime from two weeks before to two weeks after her due date.

By the fourth week, the placenta has developed and begun to function as a medium of exchange between the circulatory system of the mother and that of the fetus. These items are distinctly separate from each other—material passes from mother to fetus and back again only through diffusion. Through the placenta, the fetus receives its food, oxygen, some hormones, and enzymes. Fetal wastes are passed into the mother's system for excretion, and the placenta also serves as a barrier to any bacteria in the mother's system (although viruses and some medications pass through).

The fetus's heart begins to beat near the twenty-second day; this can be seen by ultrasound visualization techniques, but it will not generally be heard until somewhere between the sixteenth and twentieth weeks.

In the fourth week of pregnancy, the embryo is a recognizable mammal. The heart is developing rapidly, and the three main sections of the brain are identifiable. Rudimentary ears and eyes are beginning to form, as is the liver. Paired swellings appear on the trunk where the arms and legs will develop.

A five-week-old embryo is about one-third of an inch long, with a definite umbilical cord and the beginnings of a nose. Primitive upper and lower jaws may be distinguished, and the outer ears are beginning to form. The heart and liver continue to grow rapidly; the arm and leg buds have lengthened, and the hands and feet are beginning to emerge from the lengthening buds. '

At the end of the second month, almost all of the internal organs are present, the embryo is an inch long, weighs a fraction of an ounce, and has clearly human external features. Eyes, ears, and jaws are prominent; limbs develop joints; fingers and toes develop; and primitive, sexless genitalia appear.

By the twelfth week, the young fetus looks human, although the head is large in proportion to the rest of the body. Nails and bones begin forming and external genitalia are recognizable as male or female. At the end of this month, the fetus is more than 3 inches long and weighs one-half to one ounce.

A sixteen-week-old fetus's face has characteristics that can be distinguished from another fetus the same age. By the end of this month, the fetus is 6.3 inches long and weighs 4 to 6 ounces.

During the next month, fine hairs appear all over the fetus's body. Some head hairs also appear. This is the month when most women first feel fetal movement. By now, the fetus is about 10 inches long and weighs 11 to 14 ounces.

At twenty-four weeks, the fetus has discernible eyebrows and eyelashes, wrinkled skin, and a lean but better-proportioned body. Now 12 inches long, it will weigh 1.5 to 1.75 pounds.

A twenty-eight-week-old fetus has red wrinkled skin covered with a greasy protective substance. It moves its arms and legs, its eyes are now open, it's 13.5 to 15 inches long, and weighs 2.3 to 3 pounds.

In the seventh and eighth month, weight gain in the fetus is dramatic as fat begins to develop under the skin. A boy's testes have started to descend into the scrotum. The fetus is now about 16 inches long, weighing about 4 pounds.

A thirty-six-week-old fetus has smoother, less red skin, has lost much of the hair previously covering the body, and has definite fingernails and toenails. The fetus is now about 18 inches long and weighs 5 pounds, 8 ounces.

By forty weeks, time for birth, the average developed baby is 20 inches long and weighs 7.5 pounds.

Childbirth

The sequence of events during which the uterus expels a baby and the afterbirth is called labor. The afterbirth is the placenta, umbilical cord, and membranes that surrounded the baby. Labor usually starts spontaneously, but may be induced by artificial means.

Labor begins with contractions of the uterus at twenty- to thirty-minute intervals, with each contraction lasting about forty seconds. At this point, the woman will feel her uterus harden and squeeze, and will experience slight pain in the small of her back at the height of the contraction. The contractions become more frequent and more painful. The entire birth process usually takes about twelve to fifteen hours for a first delivery; subsequent births may be less than half as long. Labor pains can be lessened by drugs or training beforehand.

Labor

Labor can be thought of in three stages: dilation, birth, and afterbirth.

Dilation During this stage while the muscular wall of the uterus contracts, the muscles of the cervix expand causing dilation. The woman's cervix dilates to a width of about four inches, with involuntary contractions of the uterus occurring every three minutes by the end of the stage, when dilation is complete. The uterus is now exerting a pressure of five pounds per square inch, pushing the baby's head through the dilated cervix into the birth canal. Toward the end of this stage, the bag containing the fetus and fluid (the amniotic sac) generally breaks, although it may break earlier. This stage generally lasts eight to fourteen hours with the first delivery; later deliveries can be much shorter.

Birth   This second stage is the actual stage of delivery. It begins when the cervix is completely dilated and ends when the baby is delivered. Uterine contractions become stronger. During this stage, the baby makes its way down the birth canal, slowly stretching the canal as it descends. The woman will feel a strong urge to bear down during this phase, which adds to the uterus's contraction and helps move things along. Discomfort becomes much worse during this phase, and many doctors will suggest a local anesthetic to numb the birth canal, since pain causes most people to tense up, which slows delivery. He may also make a small incision on one side of the birth canal to prevent tearing. First babies should not take much more than an hour or so to make the journey; later children may take thirty minutes to only moments.

Newborn babies should not be expected to be beautiful! They are usually covered with a greasy, white protective coating and some blood, and their heads may be temporarily misshapen from the birth. In a very short time, everything will be cleaned up and will straighten itself out.

Afterbirth   The last stage of birth occurs when the placenta and other materials in the uterus are expelled by continuing contractions. This stage generally lasts ten to fifteen minutes.

Presentation and Delivery

Presentation refers to the part of the infant's body that appears first at the cervical opening. Usually a baby's head is born first, followed by its shoulders. Since the head is the largest part of the baby, this type of delivery is the easiest and fastest. However, the buttocks (breech presentation), the side (transverse presentation), the shoulder, the feet or the cord may appear first. These presentations may cause complications during childbirth.

Breech deliveries occur when any part of the baby's lower half is born first—something that happens in one out of thirty births. This type of birth is slower, with more danger for the baby, but most breech births are delivered with no problems. As with transverse positioning, where the baby is lying sideways, the doctor may be able to turn the baby before the head is engaged or he may elect to do a Cesarean section.

Cesarean section—In this form of delivery, the doctor makes an incision in the abdominal cavity and uterus and lifts the baby through it. Cesareans are usually done only if the mother's pelvis is too narrow, if she is ill, if there is a placental abnormality, or in an emergency situation that requires that the baby be delivered immediately.

It is important that both the mother and the father learn as much as possible about the birth process and breathing and relaxation techniques. These are extremely helpful and well worth learning. The sharing of the experience of birth can be a very meaningful time for parents. Their first glimpse of their child is a highlight of the thrill of parenthood.

Our future lies with our children. We all want to give them the best possible chance in life. The facts presented in this book are among the most important in the world. The more we make them the subject of nurturing of our children, the better it is for mankind. We have already noted that sexuality cannot be considered apart from parenthood. They go hand and hand. It is not by accident that there is a correlation from 1965 to 1985 between the percentage of births to unwed mothers and percentage of single-parent families. Births of unwed mothers rose from 7.7 to 22 percent and percentage of single-parent families from 10.1 to 22.2.

There is no more important thing we can do for the future of our children and the future of mankind than to prepare them for parenthood. Helping them understand and adjust to their sexuality is a necessary and satisfying step in that direction.

Glossary

Abortion: Expulsion of a fetus resulting in termination of pregnancy because of disruption of the fetal-placental unit variously defined as within 90 days (12 weeks, 3 months) (*see* legal *Induced abortion*) or during the first 28 weeks of pregnancy.

Spontaneous abortion—termination resulting because of an intrinsic defect or inadequate development so that the fetus can not be maintained, internal factors alone result in the loss of the fetus (*see* **Miscarriage**) expulsion may occur after fetus is nonviable (*see* **Stillbirth**).

Induced abortion—termination of pregnancy intentionally caused by external factors such as chemical or mechanical means. (Induced abortions during the first 3 months of pregnancy are legal in the United States.)

Abstinence: Voluntarily refraining from sexual intercourse.

Abuse, sexual: Any touching, talking, viewing, exposing, or overt sex act which violates the privacy and personal rights of another individual.

Amnion: A thin membrane forming a sac surrounding the developing fetus containing a watery fluid.

Anatomy: The structural makeup of the body or any of its parts.

Areola: The circular area of more pigmented skin on the breast centered around the nipple, it enlarges and darkens during puberty and pregnancy.

Bartholin's glands: Glands on either side of the vaginal opening which secrete a lubricating fluid during sexual arousal.

149

Birth control pill: A pill containing hormones taken daily which suppress ovarian function, prevent ovulation, and thereby prevent conception.

Celibacy: The state of remaining unmarried and abstaining from sexual intercourse.

Cervix: The neck or narrow end of the uterus through which the canal passes that connects the uterine cavity with the vagina.

Chastity: Abstaining from sexual intercourse outside marriage.

Circumcision: Removal of the foreskin (prepuce) of the penis, may be done based on preference or as a religious rite, usually performed in the newborn but can be done at any age. In some cultures, the clitoris was circumcised.

Clitoris: A small organ located between the upper end of the labia of the female genitalia, it contains erectile tissue, has a glans, and is richly supplied with nerve endings so it is sensitive to touch, it is the female counterpart of the penis.

Coitus: Physical act of uniting male and female genitals, sexual intercourse (also called copulation).

Conception: The beginning or inception of pregnancy, the union of a sperm and a egg.

Condom: A sheath, usually made of latex rubber, worn over the penis during intercourse to prevent conception or infection with sexually transmitted diseases.

Contraception: The deliberate prevention of conception using a variety of methods (chemical, mechanical, hormonal) which preclude or prevent the union of sperm and egg.

Contractions (labor): Painful tightening or spasms of uterine muscles (labor pains) immediately before, during, and after delivery. These contractions force the infant out through the dilated uterine cervix and vagina. After delivery, contractions continue causing delivery of the afterbirth (placenta) and clamping of the blood vessels to stop bleeding.

Copulation: Sexual intercourse, coitus.

Diaphragm: A rubber disc which is individually fitted to be placed over the cervix and used as a contraceptive device during intercourse to prevent the sperm from entering the uterine cavity.

Ejaculation: The sudden ejection or emission of semen through the male reproductive ducts and out of the penis, usually at the peak of sexual excitement and accompanied by an orgasm.

Ejaculatory duct: The duct from which semen is ejaculated, it is formed by the junction of the seminal vesicle duct and the vas deferens, passes into the prostate where it empties into the urethra.

Embryo: The term used to refer to a developing animal or human being at conception. In the human this term is used until about three months of gestation, thereafter the term fetus is used.

Epididymis: The convoluted tube attached to and lying along the testis which receive sperm from the testes, store them as they mature, and transport them to the vas deferens.

Erection: The state of firmness and rigidity of the penis or clitoris resulting from dilatation of cavernous spaces by trapped blood, a result of sexual excitement. Erection of the penis makes sexual intercourse possible.

Estrogen: A female sex hormone that stimulates and maintains female sex characteristics.

Fallopian tubes (oviducts): A pair of tubes that lead from the ovary to either side of the uterus. After ovulation the egg is carried through this tube, and if impregnation occurs it often occurs within the tube.

Fertilization: The union of an egg and a sperm initiating the development of a new individual (conception), fertilization results in pregnancy.

Fetus: The term used to refer to an unborn child as it develops in the uterus from three months after conception until birth, prior to that it is called an embryo.

Foreskin: The fold of skin surrounding the glans penis, it has been removed in the circumcised male. Also, the fold of skin over the clitoris.

Gender identity: The concept that an individual has of him/herself as a male or female, components include recognition of biologic sex, general cultural behavioral roles, and sexual roles.

Gestation (pregnancy): Period of time of pregnancy from conception until birth, approximately 40 weeks for humans.

Glans: The glans penis is the conical head of the penis made up of spongy erectile tissue and containing sensitive nerve endings, the urethra opens at the tip of the glans penis: the tip of the clitoris is also a glans.

Gonads: Reproductive sex glands which produce hormones and germ cells. The male gonad is the testis, the germ cells are sperm, the female gonad is the ovary and the cells are eggs.

Homosexual: A term used to describe a person whose choice for sexual activity is another person of the same sex.

Hormone: A chemical substance produced by cells in one part of the body which regulate or control activity in another part.

Hymen: A fold of mucus membrane which may partially cover the entrance to the vaginal canal.

Implantation: The process of attachment of the embryo to the uterine lining after which the placenta forms.

Impotence: Inability of the male to perform sexual intercourse often because of inability to achieve or maintain an erection, also sometimes used to indicate inability to impregnate or sterility in a male.

Impregnation: Onset of pregnancy (*see* **Fertilize** and **Conception**).

Infertility: The inability to conceive or beget children, defined medically as lack of conception after one year of regular intercourse without contraception.

Insemination: Placement of semen into the genital tract of a female. (**Artificial insemination:** Placement of semen by mechanical instruments into the uterus.)

Intercourse: Sexual union of male and female in which the penis penetrates the vagina (*see* **Coitus, Copulation, Sexual intercourse**).

Intrauterine device (IUD): A device inserted into the uterus (a ring, bow, loop, or spiral made of plastic, metal, or nylon) to prevent the development of an embryo. This device prevents implantation rather than conception.

In vitro fertilization: Process whereby an egg is fertilized by sperm outside the body as in a sterile laboratory dish, the fertilized egg is then placed in the uterus of the woman desiring pregnancy. The egg may be her own or donated. Likewise the sperm may be from the father/husband or donated.

Labia: The lips that comprise a portion of female genitals. There are two pairs, an outer, or major (labia majora), covered with pubic hair, and an inner (labia minora).

Masturbation: Physical stimulation of the male or female sex organs to produce pleasure, may result in orgasm, often refers to self-stimulation.

Menarche: During puberty, the first menstrual period marking the onset of menstruation.

Menopause: The cessation of menstruating which is the end of the reproductive cycle in the female, when menstruation ceases.

Menses (Menstruation): The monthly discharge of blood and uterine lining (endometrium) from the uterus occurring between puberty and menopause, except during pregnancy.

Miscarriage: Expulsion of the fetus before it is viable (spontaneous abortion), usually referring to loss occurring between 12 and 28 weeks of gestation (*see* **Stillbirth**).

Molestation, child: The seeking of sexual gratification from inappropriate viewing, exposing, touching, or sex act by an adult from a minor, a crime even if no sex act is committed.

Mucus: The secretion of the mucus glands found at various places in the body.

Nocturnal emission: Involuntary discharge of semen during sleep.

Orgasm: Intense physical sensation of pleasure and release resulting from sexual stimulation.

Ovary: The female sex glands that produce eggs (ova) and sex hormones.

Ovulation: The release of a ripe egg from the ovary which occurs monthly in healthy reproductive-aged women about midway between two menstrual periods. The egg (ova) matures in a fluid-filled follicle that bursts at ovulation.

Ovum (plural—ova): The female egg or female germ cell.

Penis: The male sex organ, an appendage through which a tube passes that drains urine from the bladder and semen during ejaculation. The penis is usually soft and limp and 3 to 4 inches long in adults, it can become erect as during sexual excitement when it becomes stiff and about 6 inches long. Referred to by a variety of slang terms.

Petting: Touching or caressing sensitive parts of the body, including passionate kissing, may be the arousal phase of sexual response.

Pornography: Any depiction of any form of erotic behavior intended to stimulate sexual excitement, may be explicit sexual conduct, real or simulated, or lewd exhibition of the genitals.

Premature ejaculation: The occurrence of ejaculation during sexual activity before desired, if ejaculation occurs early during or before intercourse actually begins or before partners are ready for the climax.

Prepuce: The fold of skin which covers the glans penis, also called the foreskin, the part removed in circumcision.

Placenta: A vascular organ consisting of maternal and fetal tissues that functions by exchange of nutrients and waste material between mother and fetus (afterbirth).

Prostate gland: A firm glandular organ containing muscle that lies just below the urinary bladder, surrounding the base of the urethra and secreting a fluid that makes up a major part of semen.

Puberty: The period during which a child matures into an adult, attaining capability of reproduction. During this time the genital organs mature, secondary sexual characteristics develop, male and female body contours mature, and menses begin in females and ejaculation in males.

Scrotum: Pouch or sac of skin suspended beneath the penis and containing the testes.

Semen: A white viscous fluid discharged through the penis at ejaculation. The fluid contains sperm in secretions of the prostate gland and seminal vesicles.

Seminal duct: The tubal system that conveys semen from the epididymis to the urethra, it is made up of the vas deferens and the ejaculatory duct.

Seminal vesicle: A pair of male accessory sex glands that open into the vas deferens just before it connects to the urethra within the prostate, secretes fluid which contributes to semen.

Sexual identity: Recognition of object of erotic pleasure-seeking as the opposite (heterosexual) or same (homosexual) sex, or both. In a sense, sexual identity is not absolute, e.g., a heterosexual male may recognize sexually stimulating circumstances involving other males. In an overall sense, most recognize a clear direction or desire.

Sexual intercourse: The physical union of the male and female genitalia with the insertion of the penis into the vagina followed by rhythmic movement usually leading to ejaculation of semen from the penis.

Sperm (Spermatozoa): The male seed or germ cell.

Sterile (infertile): A term used for individuals who are unable to reproduce, females who do not produce eggs, or males who produce no or few sperm.

Sterilization: Any surgical operation or other process that induces sterility. See tubal ligation or vasectomy.

Stillbirth: Birth of a fetus that shows no evidence of life after 28 weeks from conception.

Testis (plural testes): Either of the pair of male sex glands that produce sperm and the male sex hormone, testosterone, after puberty, also called testicle.

Tubal ligation: Procedure in which both fallopian tubes are tied and a section removed as a birth control procedure, produces sterilization.

Umbilical cord: Cord containing blood vessels which connect the fetus through the navel to the placenta, two arteries carry blood to the placenta and one vein returns it to the fetus, the umbilical cord is ensheathed by the amnion.

Urethra: Tube that connects the bladder to the exterior. In the female, it is relatively short, opens within the vulva between the clitoris and vagina, and only used for urination. In the male, it is also used for the passage of semen receiving secretions of the prostate and seminal vesicle and sperm from the vas deferens.

Uterus: The hollow organ with a muscular wall that contains and nourishes the fetus before birth, also called womb, the upper part is connected to two fallopian tubes, the lower part joins the vagina at the cervix.

Vagina: A muscular tube that connects the cervix of the uterus to the outside. Receives the penis during intercourse and serves as the birth canal.

Vas deferens: The small muscular thick walled pair of ducts which carry sperm from the testes to the urethra.

Vasectomy: A surgical procedure in which a section of each vas deferens is cut and removed to create sterility, should be considered a permanent birth control method since reversal surgery can not be assured.

Vulva: The external female genitals, consisting primarily of the 2 pairs of labia.

Reading List

Berry, Joy. *Alerting Kids to the Danger of Sexual Abuse*. Waco, Texas: Word, Educational Products Division, 1984.

Chesser, Eustace. *Love Without Fear*. New York: New American Library, 1947.

Cooper, Darien B. *You Can Be the Wife of a Happy Husband*. Wheaton, Ill.: Scripture Press, 1974.

Dennis, Muriel, ed. *Chosen Children*. Westchester, Ill.: Good News, 1978.

Dobson, James. *Hide or Seek*. Old Tappan, N.J.: Fleming H. Revell Co., 1974.

————. *Preparing for Adolescence*. Santa Ana, Calif.: Vision House, 1978.

————. *What Wives Wish Their Husbands Knew About Women*. Wheaton, Ill.: Tyndale House Publishers, Inc., 1975.

Duin, Julia. *Purity Makes the Heart Grow Stronger: Sexuality and the Single Christian*. Ann Arbor, Mich.: Servant, 1989.

The Encyclopedia of Christian Marriage. Old Tappan, N.J.: Fleming H. Revell Co., 1984.

Everywoman's Health by 17 Women Doctors. New York: Doubleday, 1980.

Family Health Guide and Medical Encyclopedia. Pleasantville, N.Y.: Reader's Digest Assn., 1970.

Fix, Janet, with Zola Levitt. *For Singles Only*. Old Tappan, N.J.: Fleming H. Revell Co., 1978.

Fried, Barbara. *The Middle-Age Crisis*. Rev. ed. New York: Harper & Row, 1976.

Hambrick-Stowe, Elizabeth A. *Expecting*. Valley Forge, Pa.: Judson, 1979.

Hatch, Claudia, ed. *What You Should Know About Sex and Sexuality*. New York: Scholastic, 1969.

Hefley, James C. *Life in the Balance*. Wheaton, Ill.: Victor Books, 1980.

Johnson, Eric W. *Love and Sex in Plain Language*. Rev. ed. Philadelphia, Pa.: J. B. Lippincott, 1977.

Kaplan, Helen Singer. *Making Sense of Sex*. New York: Simon & Schuster, 1979.

Ketterman, Grace H., M.D. *Before and After the Wedding Night*. Old Tappan, N.J.: Fleming H. Revell Co., 1984.

―――. *The Complete Book of Baby and Child Care*. Old Tappan, N.J.: Fleming H. Revell Co., 1982.

―――. *How to Teach Your Children About Sex*. Old Tappan, N.J.: Fleming H. Revell Co., 1981.

Kirk, Jerry. *The Homosexual Crisis in the Mainline Churches*. Nashville, Tenn.: Thomas Nelson, Inc., 1978.

Koop, C. Everett. *The Right to Live: The Right to Die*. Wheaton, Ill.: Tyndale, 1976.

LaHaye, Tim and Beverly. *The Act of Marriage*. Grand Rapids, Mich.: Zondervan, 1976.

Lee, Robert, and Marjorie Casebier. *The Spouse Gap*. Nashville, Tenn.: Abingdon Press, 1971.

Leman, Dr. Kevin. *Sex Begins in the Kitchen*. Ventura, Calif.: Regal Books, 1981.

Lieberman, E. James, M.D., and Ellen Peck. *Sex and Birth Control: A Guide for the Young*. Rev. ed. New York: Harper & Row, 1981.

McDowell, Josh, and Paul Lewis. *Givers, Takers and Other Kinds of Lovers*, Wheaton, Ill.: Tyndale House, 1980.

Martin, Ralph. *Husbands, Wives, Parents, Children*. Ann Arbor, Mich.: Servant, 1978.

Mayhall, Jack and Carole. *Marriage Takes More Than Love*. Colorado Springs, Colo: NAV Press, 1978.

Meredith, Don. *Becoming One*. Nashville, Tenn.: Thomas Nelson, Inc., 1979.

Miles, Herbert J. *Sexual Happiness in Marriage*. Grand Rapids, Mich.: Zondervan, 1982.

―――. *Sexual Understanding Before Marriage*. Grand Rapids, Mich.: Zondervan, 1971.

Olsen, Arvis J. *Sexuality, Guide for Teenagers*. Grand Rapids, Mich.: Baker Book House, 1981.

Penner, Clifford and Joyce. *The Gift of Sex*. Waco, Texas: Word Books, 1981.

Petersen, J. Allan. *The Marriage Affair*. Wheaton, Ill.: Tyndale House Publishers, 1971.

Rainer, Jerome and Julia. *Sexual Pleasure in Marriage*. New York: Simon & Schuster, 1969.

Rice, Shirley. *Physical Unity in Marriage*. Norfolk, Va.: The Tabernacle Church of Norfolk, 1973.

Roberts, Douglas. *To Adam With Love*. Old Tappan, N.J.: Fleming H. Revell Co., 1974.

Roetzer, Josef, M.D. *Family Planning the Natural Way*. Old Tappan, N.J.: Fleming H. Revell Co., 1981.

Small, Dwight Hervey. *Your Marriage Is God's Affair*. Old Tappan, N.J.: Fleming H. Revell Co., 1979.

Sproul R. G. *Discovering the Intimate Marriage*. Minneapolis, Minn.: Bethany House Publishers, 1981.

Stafford, Tim. *A Love Story*. Grand Rapids, Mich.: Zondervan, 1977.

Swindoll, Charles R. *Strike the Original Match*. Portland, Ore.: Multnomah Press, 1980.

Timmons, Tim. *Maximum Marriage*. Old Tappan, N.J.: Fleming H. Revell Co., 1976.

Trobisch, Ingrid, and Elisabeth Roetzer. *An Experience of Love*. Old Tappan, N.J.: Fleming H. Revell Co., 1981.

Trobisch, Walter. *I Loved a Girl*. San Francisco: Harper & Row, 1963.

Wessel, Helen. *The Joy of Natural Childbirth*. San Francisco: Harper & Row, 1976.

Wheat, Ed, M.D., and Gaye Wheat. *Intended for Pleasure*. Rev. ed. Old Tappan, N.J.: Fleming H. Revell Co., 1981.

Wooden, Kenneth. *Child Lures. A Guide for the Prevention of Molestation and Abduction*. Shelburne, Vt.: The Wooden Publishing House, 1986.

Index

Gender identity, 30 (*see* sexual identity)
Gender roles, 30
Genitalia
  proper names, 24, 68
  female, 113–115, 123
  nerve supply, 115
Glans penis, 103
Growth, 123, 124
Guilt, 66

Hernia, 106
Holy, 53, 69, 75
Homosexuality, 54–64
  and the Christian, 56, 57
  conditioning, 61
  definition, 54
  encounters, 62, 63
  factors, 59, 62
  feelings of, 58
  activities, 55
  tendencies, 58, 64
  inappropriate advances, 64
Humor, 70, 80

Indiscretions, 66
Indiscriminate sex, 77
  consequences, 78, 80
Individuality, 96
Indulgence, 66
Infertility, 133
Inhibitions, 67
Innuendos, 69
Intercourse, 29, 77, 78, 81, 88, 91, 92
  age first, 79
  child's unbelief, 21
  phases of sexual response, 88–93
  significance, 77, 78, 81
Intimacy, 58
  physical, 77
Intrauterine device (IUD), 131
Introitus, 115
In vitro fertilization, 134

Labia majora, 113, 114
Labia minora, 114, 123
Labor, 146, 147
Life history, natural sexual, 93, 94
Living together, 75
Lubricating glands
  female, 115
  male, 109

Marriage, 83–86, 94–96
  and Christ, 75, 76, 95

and Paul, 95
Marriage ceremony, 84
Marriage vow, 85
Mass media, 80
Masturbation, 41, 46–53
  acceptability, 52, 53
  and the Christian, 52, 53
  condemnation, 47, 48
  definition, 46
  and fantasy, 51
  first experience, 51
  first knowledge, 47
  guilt, 50
  historical perspective, 47–49
  incidence, 41
  negative effects, 50
  physical harm, 49
  reasons for or against, 52
  thoughts during, 53
  when wrong, 53
Menstruation, 26, 124
Menstrual cycle, 117–119
  first, 40, 124
Menopause, 122
Minimizing sex, 79
Molestation, child abusers, 28, 42–44, 63, 64
Money, 96
Monogamy, 96
Moral values, 23

Naive, 63
Natural family planning, 132
Natural sexual development, 44
Nocturnal emission, 109
Nudity, 33, 39

Onanism, 48
Offenders, 43
Oneness, 78
Openness, 24, 34, 66
Orgasm, 36, 92, 109
Ovary, 121, 122
Oviducts, 120, 121
Ovulation, 118–122, 124

Parent-child relationship, 16
  openness, 34
  social pressure, 31
  support, 111, 112
  trust factor, 32
Penis, 101–103
  nerve supply, 101–103